BOOK 3

KEY STAGE 3
Mathematics
FOR NORTHERN IRELAND

James Boston
Kate Johnston
Audrey Moody

Series Editor Miriam McMullan
Series Consultant Lowry Johnston

Acknowledgement

The Publishers would like to thank the following for permission to reproduce copyright material:
Extract from timetable for 116 on page 120 reproduced with kind permission of Translink.
Every effort has been made to trace all copyright holders, but if any have been inadvertently overlooked the Publishers will be pleased to make the necessary arrangements at the first opportunity.

Although every effort has been made to ensure that website addresses are correct at time of going to press, Hodder Education cannot be held responsible for the content of any website mentioned in this book. It is sometimes possible to find a relocated web page by typing in the address of the home page for a website in the URL window of your browser.

Hachette's policy is to use papers that are natural, renewable and recyclable products and made from wood grown in sustainable forests. The logging and manufacturing processes are expected to conform to the environmental regulations of the country of origin.

Orders: please contact Bookpoint Ltd, 130 Milton Park, Abingdon, Oxon OX14 4SB. Telephone: (44) 01235 827720. Fax: (44) 01235 400454. Lines are open 9.00 – 5.00, Monday to Saturday, with a 24-hour message answering service. Visit our website at www.hoddereducation.co.uk

© James Boston, Kate Johnston, Audrey Moody, Miriam McMullan 2008
First published in 2008 by
Hodder Education,
Part of Hachette Livre UK
338 Euston Road
London NW1 3BH

Impression number   5   4   3   2   1
Year   2012   2011   2010   2009   2008

All rights reserved. Apart from any use permitted under UK copyright law, no part of this publication may be reproduced or transmitted in any form or by any means, electronic or mechanical, including photocopying and recording, or held within any information storage and retrieval system, without permission in writing from the publisher or under licence from the Copyright Licensing Agency Limited. Further details of such licences (for reprographic reproduction) may be obtained from the Copyright Licensing Agency Limited, Saffron House, 6-10 Kirby St, London EC1N 8TS

Cover photo © Cocoon/Getty
Illustrations by Peters and Zabransky Ltd and Stephen May.
Typeset in Futura Book 11/14pt by Starfish Design Editorial and Project Management Ltd
Printed and bound in Italy

A catalogue record for this title is available from the British Library

ISBN: 978 0340 92714 4

Contents

	Introduction	iv
1	Data	2
2	Angles	12
	● Task 1 Angles and Polygons	21
3	Calculation and Number	23
4	Algebra	33
5	3-D Shape	43
6	Decimals	53
7	Ratio and Proportion	63
8	Patterns and Sequences	71
	● Task 2 Sequences	80
9	Measures 1	82
	● Task 3 Planning a Garden	91
10	Fractions, Decimals and Percentages 1	92
11	Measures 2	102
	● Task 4 Waste Reduction	111
12	Time	112
13	Mass	121
14	Fractions, Decimals and Percentages 2	132
	● Task 5 Standby	142
15	Negative Numbers	144
16	Probability	153
	● Task 6 Take Your Pick	162
	Index	163

Introduction

This series has been written specifically for the Key Stage 3 Curriculum for Northern Ireland.

Book 3 provides opportunities to develop the mathematical skills and understanding you will need if you are working at Level 5 of the Progression in Using Mathematics across the Curriculum levels (with the introduction of a number of Level 6 topics). This is achieved through a wide variety of learning approaches, including discussions, examples, exercises, consolidation practice, practical activities and Tasks.

This Pupil's Book provides opportunities to:

- Cover the Key Elements for Mathematics with Financial Capability.
- Develop Thinking Skills and Personal Capabilities.
- Develop the skill of Using ICT.
- Develop Mental Mathematics skills.
- Complete exercises with and without using a calculator.

Key Elements

The Key Elements for Mathematics with Financial Capability in Book 3 are met in the following ways.

1	Personal understanding	• Investigate ways in which we spend our time.
2	Mutual understanding	• Show respect for others' views when working in a group or in class discussions.
3	Personal health	• Investigate how choices about food and exercise affect our health. • Carry out experiments and analyse data relating to health issues.
4	Moral character	• Provide a reasoned solution to questions.
5	Spiritual awareness	• Investigate patterns in nature.
6	Citizenship	• Find out how you can get involved in issues that affect your school, your local area and the wider world through mathematical data.
7	Cultural understanding	• Explore the contributions of different cultures to mathematics.
8	Media awareness	• Examine the use and misuse of mathematics in the media. • Interpret data used by the media.

9	Ethical awareness	•	Look at statistics in relation to social issues.
10	Employability	• •	Examine the role of mathematics as a 'key' to your future education, training and employment. Explore how the skills developed through mathematics will be useful in a range of careers.
11	Economic awareness	•	Apply mathematical skills in real-life situations linking with financial capability.
12	Education for sustainable development	• •	Understand the need to manage renewable and non-renewable resources. Investigate the various costs and benefits of waste management.

The opportunities for the key elements of Thinking Skills and Personal Capabilities are indicated by the following icons.

Skill	Icon	Description
Managing information		• Research and manage information relating to mathematical situations, including collecting and recording primary data, interpreting a range of secondary sources such as tables, charts, diagrams and graphs. • Analyse and carry out calculations for sets of data and present findings using paper methods or with ICT packages.
Thinking, problem solving, decision making		• Show deeper mathematical understanding by generating possible outcomes, suggesting alternative approaches and evaluating methods chosen. • Make links with mathematical knowledge and other situations.
Being creative		• Develop the ability to generate appropriate questions to define problems and be able to suggest a variety of strategies for their solution. • Develop the individual's confidence in his or her approach.
Working with others		• Work effectively in pairs or in a group, valuing the contribution of others.
Self-management		• Work independently to manage, evaluate and improve own learning.

1 Data

In this chapter, I am learning to:
- interpret information from pie charts
- draw pie charts
- calculate the mean and range of a set of data.

Discussion 1.1

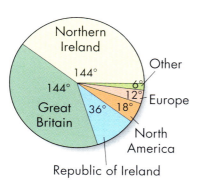

Adam is doing a survey about visitors to Northern Ireland. He asks 120 visitors to the Giant's Causeway which country they are from. He draws a pie chart to show his results. Why is this a suitable method to use to present his results?
Using the angles of the pie chart we can work out how many visitors came from each of the countries.

The section for Northern Ireland is represented by 144°.

The fraction of the whole pie chart for Northern Ireland is $\frac{144}{360}$. (Why 360?)

$\frac{144}{360}$ can be cancelled down to $\frac{2}{5}$.

$\frac{2}{5}$ of the visitors were from Northern Ireland. There were 120 visitors altogether so the number from Northern Ireland was $\frac{2}{5}$ of 120.

$120 \div 5 \times 2 = 48$

48 visitors were from Northern Ireland.

Work in pairs. Copy and complete the table below.

Country	Angle on pie chart	Fraction	Simplified fraction	Number of people
N. Ireland	144°	$\frac{144}{360}$	$\frac{2}{5}$	48
Republic of Ireland	36°			
Great Britain	144°			
Europe	12°			
N. America	18°			
Other	6°			

Exercise 1a

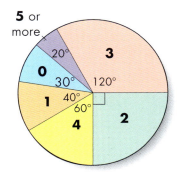

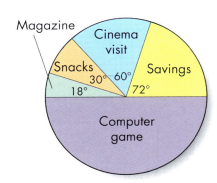

McClure family

Williams family

1 Angela asked 36 Year 8 pupils how many portions of fruit and vegetables they had eaten the day before. Her results are shown in the pie chart.

Copy and complete the table to show how many pupils ate each number of portions of fruit and vegetables.

Number of portions	Angle	Fraction	Simplified fraction	Number of pupils
0				
1				
2				
3				
4				
5 or more				

2 Sam was given £60 for his birthday. The pie chart shows how he spent his money.

Copy and complete the table to calculate how much Sam spent on each item.

Item	Angle	Fraction	Simplified fraction	Money spent
Computer game				
Savings				
Cinema visit				
Snacks				
Magazine				

3 The first pie chart shows how the McClure family spent £60 on food shopping.

   a How much money did they spend on
      i Ready meals   ii Fruit and vegetables?

   b The second pie chart shows how the Williams family spent £72 on food shopping.

      How much money did they spend on
      i Ready meals   ii Fruit and vegetables?

   c The Williams and McClure families spent the same amount on Meat and fish.

      (£12 – you can check this if you want to.) Why are the angles different on the pie charts?

Example 1.1

Alex asked 60 Year 10 pupils how they travelled to school in the mornings.

The results are shown in the table.

Method of travel	Number of pupils
School Bus	30
Service Bus	18
Car	6
Walk	3
Taxi	3

To draw a pie chart for Alex's data, we first need to calculate the size of the angles for each method of transport. A table similar to the one in the last exercise is useful.

Method of travel	Number of pupils	Fraction	Simplified fraction	Angle
School Bus	30	$\frac{30}{60}$	$\frac{1}{2}$	180°
Service Bus	18	$\frac{18}{60}$	$\frac{3}{10}$	108°
Car	6			
Walk	3			
Taxi	3			

The fraction for pupils travelling by School Bus is $\frac{30}{60} = \frac{1}{2}$

To find the angle for the School Bus we need to find $\frac{1}{2}$ of 360° and 360 ÷ 2 = 180. We need to draw an angle of 180° to represent the number of pupils who take the School Bus.

To work out the angle for the Service Bus

- first write down the fraction of pupils ($\frac{18}{60}$)

- simplify this ($\frac{3}{10}$)

- find this fraction of 360 (360 ÷ 10 × 3 = 108°).

We need to draw an angle of 108° to represent the number of pupils who take the Service Bus.

Exercise 1b

SUS1b

1. Complete the table on SUS1b to find all the angles for Alex's pie chart.

2. Amy spent 2 hours doing her homework one night. The number of minutes she spent on each subject is shown in the table.

Subject	Number of minutes
Maths	40
English	20
French	20
Art	10
Geography	30

   Complete the table on SUS1b to show the angles required for a pie chart.

3. Andrew has saved £120 to spend on tennis equipment. He spends £90 on a racquet, £18 on a sports bag, £6 on tennis balls and £6 on a T-shirt.

   Draw table like the ones on SUS1b to show the angles needed to draw a pie chart for this information.

4. The manager of a coffee shop records which sort of coffee 200 customers have bought.

   This data is shown in the table.

Type of coffee	Number bought
Regular	80
Cappuccino	50
Latte	40
Americano	20
Frappaccino	10

   Calculate the angles that would be needed to draw a pie chart for this data.

SUS Example 1.2

Example 1.2

When the sizes of the angles are calculated we can draw the pie charts. The instructions for drawing the pie chart for Example 1.1 are shown below.

- The first angle we need to draw is 180°, so draw a horizontal line straight across the circle.

- The next angle is 108°. Put the line at the bottom of your protractor along the horizontal line you have just drawn and draw an angle of 108°.

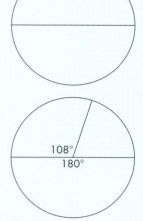

- The next angle is 36°. Continue as before, using the radius you have just drawn to put the base line of your protractor against.

- Now draw an angle of 18° from your new radius.

- You do not have to draw the last angle as you should be back to the starting line. You should check that it is about 18°.

- Now label the sectors of the pie chart. You do not need to mark the angles on it.

- Give your pie chart a title – 'Method of Transport to School'.

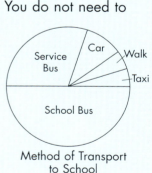

Method of Transport to School

Exercise 1c

Draw the pie charts for the rest of the questions in Exercise 1b.

Activity 1.1

Discussion 1.2

The statements below are all taken from recent newspaper articles.

The average weight of a newborn baby in this country is 7.5 lbs (3405 g).

The average attendance at Manchester United's home matches was 75 826 for the 2006/7 season.

Cats live for 14 years on average.

What do you think 'average' means?

Why might we want to know the average weight of a newborn baby or the average attendance at Manchester United or the average life of a cat?

Can you think of any other averages that might be useful to know?

One way of calculating an average is to find the mean.

To find the **mean** of a set of values add all the values together to find the total, then divide the total by the number of values.

Example 1.3

Sheila records how many minutes it takes to get to work each day for one week.

Monday – 16 minutes
Tuesday – 14 minutes
Wednesday – 12 minutes
Thurday –13 minutes
Friday –10 minutes

Find the mean time for Sheila to get to work.

- Add all the values together: 16 + 14 + 12 + 13 + 10 = 65.
- Divide the total by the number of values.

There are five values so 65 ÷ 5 = 13

The average time taken is 13 minutes.

Exercise 1d

1. Naomi recorded how much money she had saved each week for six weeks.

   £3.50   £3.20   £1.80   £2.40   £3.00   £2.30

   Find the mean amount that Naomi saved per week.

2. **a** Ryan asks a group of five friends how many texts they had sent the previous day. These are the results.

   12   9   3   14   12

   What is the mean number of texts sent by this group of friends?

   b Ryan asks another group of five friends how many texts they had sent the previous day. These are the results.

   2   0   5   3   5

   What is the mean number of texts sent by this group of friends?

   c One of the groups was made up completely of girls and the other was made up completely of boys.

   Which group do you think was which? Give a reason for your answer.

3. The manager of a leisure centre recorded how many customers used the leisure centre on weekdays during a particular week.

Day	Monday	Tuesday	Wednesday	Thursday	Friday
Number of customers	147	238	189	201	165

   Find the mean number of customers visiting the leisure centre per day.

4. The table shows the heights and weights of eight members of a female rowing team.

	Jane	Lesley	Siobhan	Beth	Kate	Maura	Ashleen	Anne
Height (cm)	175	164	170	161	168	170	165	163
Weight (kg)	67	61	70	58	65	62	65	64

   a Find the mean height of the rowers.

   b Find the mean weight of the rowers.

The **range** of a set of values tells us how much the data varies.

The range of a set of data is the difference between the highest and the lowest value.

Example 1.4

The table shows the daytime temperature in Sydney and Belfast in one week.

Day	Mon	Tues	Wed	Thur	Fri	Sat	Sun
Temperature in Sydney (°C)	29	32	30	28	29	31	29
Temperature in Belfast (°C)	11	15	16	9	11	13	9

The **range** of the temperatures for Sydney tells us how much the temperature varied over the week.

Range = highest temperature − lowest temperature

32° − 28° = 4°

The range of the temperatures for Sydney was 4°C.

Exercise 1e

1. Find the range of temperature for Belfast from the table in Example 1.4.

2. The heights of six male professional basketball players are as follows.

   210 cm   215 cm   208 cm   217 cm   212 cm   218 cm

   Find the range of heights for these players.

3. The heights of six male bank managers are as follows.

   173 cm   191 cm   178 cm   180 cm   169 cm   181 cm

   a. Find the range of heights for these bank managers.

   b. Why do you think the range is much higher for the bank managers than for the basketball players from Question 2?

4 The table shows how much money Year 9 classes collected for charity.

9E	9L	9M	9G	9D
£30.56	£47.43	£38.72	£23.92	£44.38

a Four of the classes have 28 pupils and one class has 17 pupils.
  i Which class do you think has 17 pupils?
  ii Give a reason for your answer.

b Find the range of the amounts collected by the Year 9 classes.

5 a Find the range of the heights of the female rowing team from Question 4 in Exercise 1d on page 8.

b Find the range of the weights of the female rowing team from Question 4 in Exercise 1d.

Activity 1.2

Consolidation Exercise 1

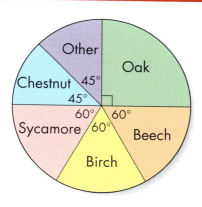

1 Alastair is doing a woodland study for a Science project.

He identifies 120 trees in a wood near his house.

He draws a pie chart to show his results.

a How many of the trees were oak trees?
b How many were sycamore trees?
c How many were chestnut trees?
d Why do you think there is a section labelled 'Other'?

2 Amy gets £72 for her birthday. She spends £24 on clothes, £18 on cosmetics and £3 on a magazine. She saves the rest.

a Copy and complete this table.

	Money spent (£s)	Fraction	Simplified fraction	Angle for pie chart
Clothes	24			
Cosmetics	18			
Magazine	3			
Saved				

b Draw a pie chart to show how Amy spent her money.

3 As part of an environmental scheme, the Murray family are recording the number of litres of water they use every day.

The table shows how many litres they used every day in the first week of the scheme.

Day	Monday	Tuesday	Wednesday	Thursday	Friday	Saturday	Sunday
Water used (litres)	651	683	627	597	694	753	769

a Why do you think more water was used on Saturday and Sunday than on weekdays?

b Find the mean number of litres of water used per day.

c Find the range of the number of litres of water used per day.

d In the same week, the mean number of litres of water used by the McMahon family was 431 litres. One of the families have three children and the other family is an elderly couple. Which family do you think has three children?

4 Rory is practising the long jump for a local athletics competition.

The lengths of his first eight jumps are

7.93 m 7.82 m 7.94 m 7.61 m

7.58 m 7.64 m 7.73 m 7.59 m.

a Find the mean length of Rory's eight jumps.

b Find the range for Rory's eight jumps.

c Rory's ninth jump was his best one. The range for all nine jumps was 2.37 m. Find the length of Rory's ninth jump.

Angles

In this chapter, I am learning to:
- recognise the relationships between angles associated with straight, intersecting and parallel lines
- understand the terms vertically opposite, alternate, corresponding and interior angles
- recognise angle properties of triangles and quadrilaterals.

Discussion 2.1

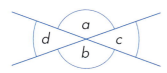

Look at the pair of intersecting lines. Angles *a* and *b* and angles *c* and *d* are known as **vertically opposite angles**. What can you say about the size of angles *a* and *b*? What about angles *c* and *d*? Use a protractor to check your answers. Will this be the case for any pair of intersecting lines? Check by drawing pairs of intersecting lines and measuring the vertically opposite angles.

Exercise 2a

1 Find the size of each of the missing angles.

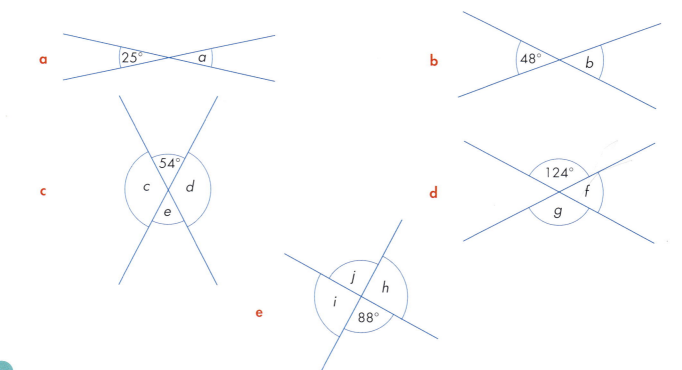

A line that cuts another set of lines is called a **transversal**. The line AB is a transversal as it cuts the other two lines.

The angles labelled p and t are **corresponding** angles. Corresponding angles are in corresponding positions with regard to the transversal and the line it cuts.

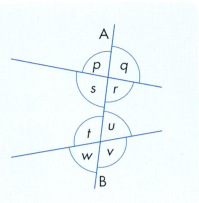

Discussion 2.2

In the information above the corresponding angles p and t are both to the left of the transversal and both lie above the line cut by the transversal. Are q and p corresponding? What about q and u? Work with a partner and find other pairs of corresponding angles. What letter of the alphabet would help you recognise corresponding angles?

Corresponding angles are equal if the lines the transversal cuts are parallel.

Activity 2.1

Exercise 2b

1 **a** Copy the diagram and mark the angle which corresponds to a. Are the corresponding angles equal? Give a reason.

   b Make another copy of the diagram and mark the angle which corresponds to b. Are the corresponding angles equal? Give a reason.

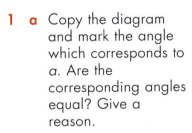

2 **a** Copy the diagram and mark the angles which correspond to a. Are the corresponding angles equal? Give a reason.

   b Make another copy of the diagram and mark the angles which correspond to b. Are the corresponding angles equal? Give a reason.

   c What do you notice about angles a and b? Explain your answer.

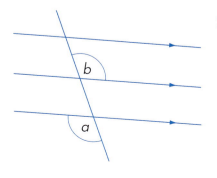

3 Find the missing angles. You will need to use your knowledge of angles and lines.

a   b   c   d

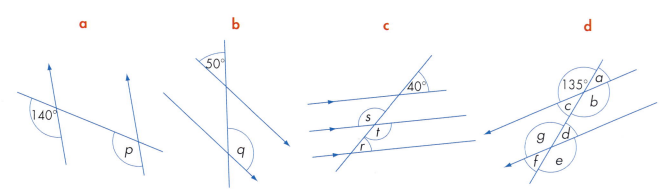

4 Find the missing angles.

a 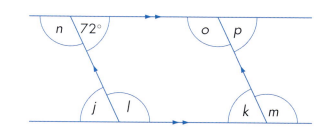   b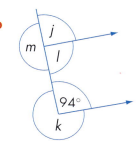

Discussion 2.3

Look at the diagram.

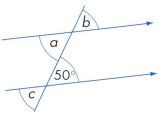

As the lines are parallel, by corresponding angles, the angle labelled *b* must be 50°. As angles *a* and *b* are vertically opposite, angle *a* must also be 50°. There is another way to work out angle *a*.

Can you see the 'Z' shape in the diagram? Use tracing paper and rotate the diagram through half a turn. Where does the angle *a* end up? What does this suggest? These angles are called **alternate** angles.

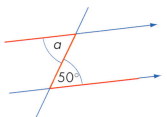

Alternate angles are equal if the lines the transversal cuts are parallel.

Exercise 2c

1 Find the missing angles. You will need to use the angle facts you have learnt so far.

a

b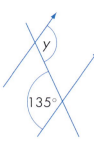

c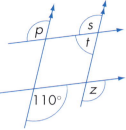

d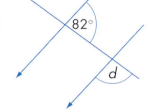

e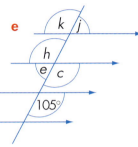

2 a State whether AB is parallel to CD. Give a reason.

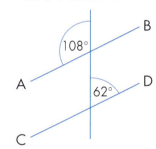

b State whether EF is parallel to GH. Give a reason.

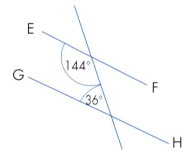

Activity 2.2

Discussion 2.4

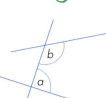

Look at the diagram.

A transversal cuts through two lines. Are the lines parallel? Angles *a* and *b* are called **interior** angles. What does interior mean? Describe another pair of interior angles in the diagram. Are the interior angles equal?

Work with a partner. Draw a pair of parallel lines each and cut these lines with a transversal. Label a pair of interior angles then measure them. What is the sum of the interior angles? Check your partner agrees with you. Write a statement to summarise your findings. Is the result the same when the pair of lines is not parallel?

Exercise 2d

1 **a** Name the two pairs of interior angles.

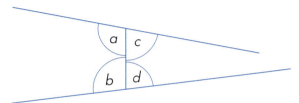

   b Are either pair of interior angles supplementary (add up to 180°)? Give a reason for your answer.

2 Find the missing angles. Give a reason for each of your answers.

a

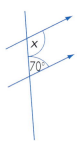

b

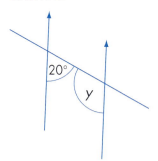

c

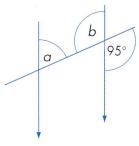

d

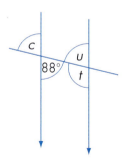

e

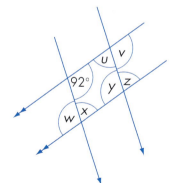

f

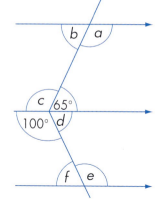

3 Describe two different methods to calculate the size of angle e.

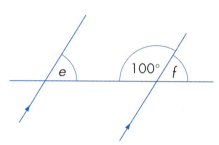

4 Is AB parallel to CD? Give a reason.

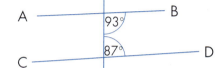

Example 2.1

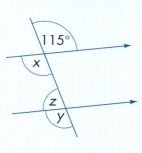

Find the missing angles. Give detailed reasons with your answer.

Angle x and 115° are vertically opposite angles, so x = 115°.

x and y are corresponding angles and are equal since the transversal crosses parallel lines, so y = 115°.

Angles y and z are supplementary angles (sum to 180°) as they form a straight line angle, so
z = 180° − 115° = 65°.

Exercise 2e

Give reasons for all answers in this exercise.

1 Find the missing angles in each of the diagrams.

a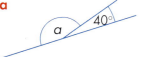

b

c

d

e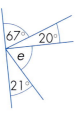

f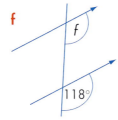

g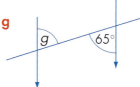

h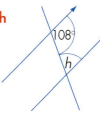

2 Find the angle between the roof and the wall.

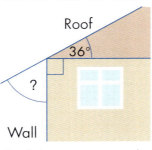

3 Find the missing angles on this pair of scissors.

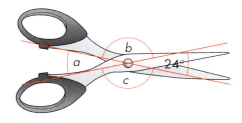

4 Find the missing angle in this pie chart.

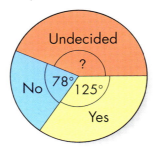

5 Calculate the values of a, b, c, d and e in the diagram.

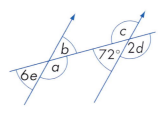

Discussion 2.5

The interior angles of a shape are the angles inside the shape. The interior angles of the triangle are labelled a, b and c.

What is the sum of the interior angles of a triangle? What size is each angle of an equilateral triangle? What size are the equal angles of a right-angled isosceles triangle? Can a triangle contain two obtuse angles? Explain your answer.

An obtuse angled isosceles triangle has a 25° angle. What size are the other angles?

The exterior angles of a shape are the angles you get if you extend the sides. What does exterior mean?

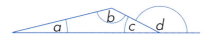

Angle d is an exterior angle of the triangle. How could you find the exterior angle if you know the size of the interior angle next to it?

Activity 2.3

Exercise 2f

1 Find the missing angles in these triangles.

   a   b

2 a Find the missing angles which follow. Give reasons for your answers.

i    ii    iii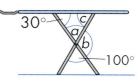

iv 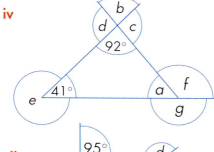   v 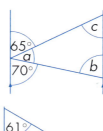   vi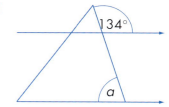

vii 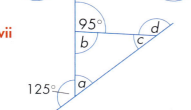 viii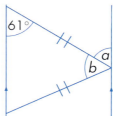

ix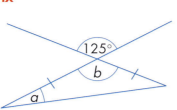

x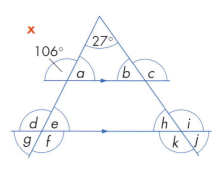

b In part **iii** is the top of the ironing board parallel to the floor? Explain your answer.

c Add the three exterior angles together in part **vii**.

d Add the exterior angles together in part **iv**. What do you notice about this answer and your previous answer for part **c**?

The angle sum of a quadrilateral is 360°.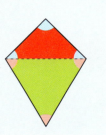

Exercise 2g

1 Name these quadrilaterals and calculate their missing angles.

a **b** **c**

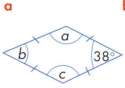 

2 Find the missing angles. Give reasons for your answers.

a **b**

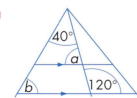 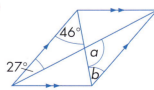

3 Three interior angles of a quadrilateral measure 72°, 87° and 129°. What size is the fourth angle?

4 One angle of a rhombus is 23°. What size is each of the other three angles?

Consolidation Exercise 1

1 Describe each of the pairs of marked angles. Choose from alternate, corresponding, vertically opposite and interior.

a  b   c   d   e

Give reasons for your answers to the rest of the questions in this exercise.

2 a Is AB parallel to CD?   b Is EF parallel to GH?

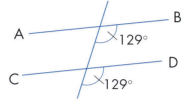

3 Find the missing angles in each of the diagrams.

a 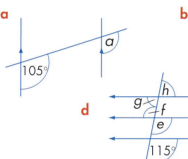 b 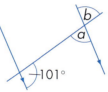 c

d (within image 8) e 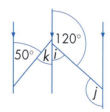 f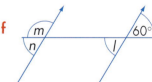

4 Find the size of the missing angles.

a   b 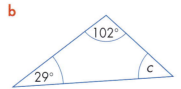 c 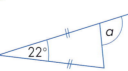 d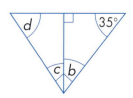

5 Find the size of the labelled interior and exterior angles for the quadrilaterals.

a 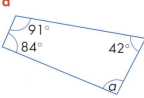 b 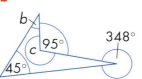 c 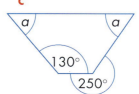 d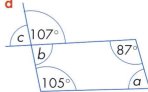

Task 1: Angles and Polygons

Part A

Draw a range of irregular polygons to include a triangle, a quadrilateral, a pentagon, a hexagon and an octagon. Measure each of the interior angles and find the angle sums of your polygons. Put your results into a table like this one.

Polygon	Angle sum
Triangle	
Quadrilateral	
Pentagon	

Compare your results with friends and discuss your findings. Did everyone get the same answers?

If not, why not?

Part B

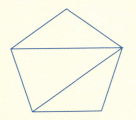

A pentagon can be split into three triangles as shown. Can it be split into two triangles?

1. What is the angle sum of a triangle?
2. What is the angle sum of three triangles?
3. What is the angle sum of a pentagon?
4. What size is each interior angle if the pentagon is regular?
5. If an interior angle is known, how could a corresponding exterior angle be found?
6. If the interior angle, a, of the pentagon shown is 108°, what size is the exterior angle, b?

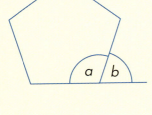

Fill in a copy of the **regular polygons table** on SUSTask1.

7. What is the exterior angle sum for each of the polygons?
8. Find a rule which generates angle sums that is true for all polygons.
9. What is the angle sum of a 20-sided polygon?
10. Write down rules to find the exterior and interior angles of regular polygons.

Part C

Some polygons, such as rectangles, will tessellate.

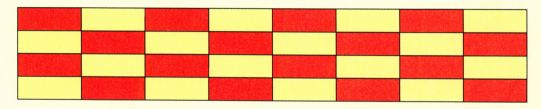

11 Which of the regular polygons will tessellate?

12 Use your table from Part B to help you find a rule to decide whether a regular polygon will tessellate.

3 Calculation and Number

> **In this chapter, I am learning to:**
> - understand and use square and cube roots
> - understand and use index notation
> - carry out calculations in the correct order (BODMAS)
> - understand lowest common multiple (LCM) and highest common factor (HCF)
> - write numbers as a product of their prime factors.

Example 3.1

4^2 is read as 4 squared. $4^2 = 4 \times 4 = 16$. 16 is a **square number**.

4^3 is read as 4 cubed. $4^3 = 4 \times 4 \times 4 = 64$. 64 is a **cube number**.

Exercise 3a

1. Write down the first ten square numbers.
2. Write down the first five cube numbers.
3. Copy and complete.

   a $8^2 = $ ____
   b ____$^3 = 64$
   c $100 = $ ____^{2}
   d $10^3 = $ ____
   e $7^2 = $ ____
   f $11^2 = $ ____
   g $3^- = 27$
   h $2^- = 8$

Example 3.2

$3 \times 3 \times 3 \times 3$ can be written as 3^4. 3^4 is read as '3 to the power of 4'.

When $3 \times 3 \times 3 \times 3$ is written as 3^4 we are using **index notation**.

The small 4 is called the **index** or the **power**.

23

Discussion 3.1

How would you write 4 × 4 × 4 × 4 × 4 × 4 in index notation?

How would you write out 3^7 fully?

What is the value of 2^4?

How would you write 5 to the power of 6?

Example 3.3

We can use a scientific calculator to find the value of numbers written in index notation.

Find 3^5

Key in:

Your display should show 243.

Exercise 3b

1 Copy and complete.

   a $7 \times 7 \times 7 \times 7 = 7^-$

   b $6 \times 6 \times 6 \times 6 \times 6 \times 6 \times 6 = 6^-$

   c 8 to the power of 7 = _____

   d 4^9 = _____ to the power of _____

   e $3^8 = 3 \times 3 \times$ _____

   f 16 = 2 to the power of _____

2 Use your scientific calculator to find the value of these.

   a 6^4 b 7^5 c 3^6 d 8^5 e 8^8 f 1^{23}

3 Put these in ascending order (smallest first).

   a $5 \times 5 \times 5$ 4^4 2 to the power of 9   6 cubed

   b 3^4 15^2 4^3 2^7

4 Which one is the odd one out?

   $10^2 \times 10^4$ 1000^2 $10\,000\,000$ 100^3 1 million

5 Copy and complete these statements by putting either > , < or = between the two numbers.

   a 2^5 4×2^3

   b 2^{11} 11^3

   c 3 to the power of 4   4 to the power of 3

Activity 3.1

Activity Sheet 3.1

Discussion 3.2

Sophie says that she has squared a number and got 64. What number did she square?

Sophie squares a different number and gets 324.

Ian says that he knows the number must be bigger than 10. Is this correct? How can you tell? How could you find out what number Sophie squared?

Example 3.4

The key can be used to find out what number has been squared. This is called finding the **square root.** Finding the square root is the inverse of squaring.

Find √324

Key in:

Answer = 18

Exercise 3c

1 Find the square root of these.

    a 400   b 1 000 000

    c 225   d 900

    e 2025   f 5041

2 Copy and complete.

    a The square root of 1089 is _____

    b 89 is the square root of _____

    c √40 000 = _____

    d √_____ = 25

    e √_____ = 19

3 Gina wants to estimate the square root of 40. She knows that √36 is 6 and √49 is 7. As 40 is between 36 and 49, Gina knows that √40 must be between 6 and 7.

Copy and complete the statements.

    a √21 is between _____ and _____.

    b √7 is between _____ and _____.

    c √88 is between _____ and _____.

    d √30 is between _____ and _____.

    e √68 is between _____ and _____.

Discussion 3.3

Josh says that he has cubed a number and got 27. What number did he cube?

Josh cubes a different number and gets 729. He knows the number must be bigger than 5.

Is he correct? How can you tell? Explain how to find the number that he cubed.

Example 3.5

The key is used to find out what number has been cubed. This is called finding the cube root. Finding the cube root is the inverse of cubing.

Use your calculator to find the cube root of 729.

Key in:

Answer = 9

Exercise 3d

1 Find the cube root of these.
   a 1000
   b 512
   c 1728
   d 216
   e 8000
   f 343

2 Copy and complete.
   a The cube root of 64 is _____
   b _____ is the cube root of 27
   c $\sqrt[3]{1\,000\,000}$ = _____
   d $\sqrt[3]{\_\_\_\_}$ = 6
   e $\sqrt[3]{\_\_\_\_}$ = 15
   f $\sqrt[3]{5832}$ = _____

3 Find the value of these.

 a $3^5 - 5^3$

 b $\sqrt[3]{2197} + \sqrt{729}$

 c $8^3 + \sqrt{1764}$

 d $2^3 \times 3^2$

 e 3 to the power of 6 plus 6 cubed.

4 Which of these statements are false?

 a The square of 25 is 625

 b The cube root of 2 is 8

 c $\sqrt{9}$ is 81

 d $2^4 = 4^2$

 e $2^6 = 2^2 \times 2^4$

 f $2^6 \div 2^2 = 2^4$

 g $2^5 > 5^2$

5 Write two false statements of your own, like those in Question 4, which you think other pupils would find difficult to answer. Why are these difficult?

Discussion 3.4

Daniel and Ann are practising mental maths. They are working out the answer to

$3 + 2 \times 5$.

Daniel says the answer is 25 and Ann says the answer is 13. Which answer is correct? Check using a calculator.

The order in which you do calculations is important. There are rules that must be followed to get the correct answer.

Always do any multiplying or dividing before you do any adding or subtracting.

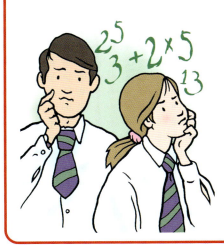

Work with a partner to find the correct answer to these. Discuss your answers and agree on the answer you think is correct.

$5 + 4 \times 2$

$3 \times 10 - 6 \times 4$

$20 - 2 \times 5 + 6$

$8 \times 4 - 6 + 4 \times 3$

The rules for the order of calculations are sometimes called 'Order of operations'.

The word BODMAS is often used to remind us of these rules.

B stands for 'brackets'. Calculations in brackets must be done first.

O stands for 'order' but really means 'powers of' or indices.

DM stands for division and multiplication. It does not matter which of these you do before the other. Work from left to right.

AS stands for addition and subtraction. It does not matter which of these you do before the other. Work from left to right.

Example 3.6

$10 \times (4 + 2) - 15 \div 3 + 4$

Do brackets first (B).

$10 \times (4 + 2) - 15 \div 3 + 4$

$10 \times 6 - 15 \div 3 + 4$

Then do the division and multiplication (DM) working from left to right.

$10 \times 6 - 15 \div 3 + 4$

$60 - 5 + 4$

Finally, addition and subtraction (AS) working from left to right.

$60 - 5 + 4 = 59$

Example 3.7

$8 + 3 \times 2^2 - 5 + (2 + 5) \times 2$

$8 + 3 \times 2^2 - 5 + (2 + 5) \times 2$	B
$8 + 3 \times 2^2 - 5 + 7 \times 2$	O
$8 + 3 \times 4 - 5 + 7 \times 2$	DM
$8 + 12 - 5 + 14 = 29$	AS

Exercise 3e

Use the rules for order of operations to find the answers to these.

1. $3 + 4 \times 6$
2. $16 - 5 \times 2$
3. $18 + 15 \div 5 - 10$
4. $5 \times 3 + 4 \times 2$
5. $20 - 3 \times 6 + 4$
6. $5 \times (4 + 3) - 11$
7. $8 + (3 \times 4) - 14 \div 2$
8. $10 + 2 \times (7 - 4) + 6$
9. $3 \times (3 + 2) + (19 - 16) \times 2$
10. $3 \times (5 - 4) + 3^2 \times 6$
11. $20 - 2^3 + (32 \div 4) - 4$
12. $8 + 5 \times 2 + 4^2 - 6 \times 3$

Activity Sheet 3.2

Activity 3.2

Discussion 3.5

What is meant by 'multiples'?

What are the first five multiples of 3?

What are the first five multiples of 4?

What is the **lowest common multiple (LCM)** of 3 and 4? How do you know this?

What is the lowest common multiple of 6 and 8?

Explain how to find the lowest common multiple (LCM) of 7 and 9.

What is meant by the lowest common multiple (LCM) of a pair of numbers?

Exercise 3f

1. **a** Write down the first five multiples of 5
   b Write down the first five multiples of 3
   c What is the first number that appears on both lists (from **a** and **b**)?

   This is the **lowest common multiple** of 5 and 3.

2. Find the LCM of these sets of numbers. Write down two lists of multiples. Continue the lists until you get the same number in both lists.

   a 6 and 9   **b** 4 and 6   **c** 5 and 11   **d** 10 and 25

Example 3.8

Factors are the numbers that divide exactly into another number.

Find the **highest common factor (HCF)** of 24 and 32

List the factors of 24

The factors of 24 are 1, 2, 3, 4, 6, 8, 12 and 24

List the factors of 32

The factors of 32 are 1, 2, 4, 8, 16 and 32

The highest number that appears in both lists is the highest common factor of 24 and 32

8 is the HCF of 24 and 32

Exercise 3g

1 a Write down all the factors of 18

   b Write down all the factors of 24

   c What is the highest number that appears in both lists? This is the highest common factor of 18 and 24

2 Find the HCF of these numbers.

   a 16 and 12

   b 10 and 25

   c 27 and 18

   d 32 and 40

   e 42 and 35

Discussion 3.6

To write a number as a product of its prime factors it is useful to use a factor tree. What is a prime number? What are the first ten prime numbers? Is 1 a prime number? Explain your answer.

What does product mean?

What do you think it means to write a number as a product of its prime factors?

Look at the factor tree for 90.

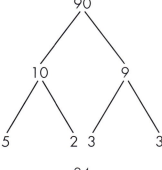

The two numbers beside each other multiply to give the number above.

The numbers at the end of the branches multiply to give the original number

$5 \times 2 \times 3 \times 3 = 90$

The numbers are usually written in order $2 \times 3 \times 3 \times 5 = 90$

or using index notation $2 \times 3^2 \times 5 = 90$

Work with a partner to copy and complete the factor tree for 24

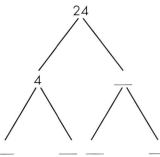

___ × ___ × ___ × ___ = 24

Write your answer using index notation.

Does it matter if you start with 2 × 12 instead of 4 × 6?

2, 3 and 5 are the **prime factors** of 90

When we say $2 \times 3^2 \times 5 = 90$, we are writing 90 as the **product of prime factors**.

Exercise 3h

Write these numbers as the product of their prime factors. Use a factor tree for each.

1 42   **2** 54   **3** 45   **4** 64   **5** 84   **6** 250   **7** 75   **8** 1000

Consolidation Exercise 1

1. Write these in index notation.
   a. 3 × 3 × 3 × 3 × 3
   b. 7 squared
   c. 10 × 10 × 10 × 10
   d. 8 cubed
   e. 9 to the power of 8

2. Use BODMAS to calculate these.
   a. 7 + 3 × 5
   b. 3 × 10 − 6 × 2
   c. (14 − 5) × 2 − 10
   d. 5 + 7 × 2 − 4 × 3
   e. 8 + 2 × (6 − 4) − 5
   f. 2 × (13 − 8) + (9 − 1) × 2
   g. 2 × (5 − 3) + 4^2 × 6
   h. 6 × 5 − 2^3 + (32 ÷ 4)
   i. 8 + 5 × 2 + 4^2 − 6 × 3
   j. 10 + 5 × (7 + 3) − 4 × 5

3. Are the following statements true or false?
   a. 81 is a prime number.
   b. All prime numbers are odd.
   c. 61 is a prime number.
   d. 91 is a prime number.
   e. There are only two prime numbers between 40 and 50.
   f. The first prime number greater than 100 is 107.

4. Write these as the product of their prime factors.
   a. 72   b. 500   c. 77   d. 650   e. 270

5. Find the value of these.
   a. 18^2 b. 7^3 c. $\sqrt{81}$ d. 6^5 e. $\sqrt[3]{216}$
   f. 3 to the power of 8   g. 8^3 h. 10^4 i. $\sqrt[3]{729000}$

4 Algebra

In this chapter, I am learning to:
- understand and use the rules of algebra
- simplify expressions
- use inverse function machines
- use substitution to find the value of expressions
- solve linear equations.

Discussion 4.1

Neil works in a café at lunchtime. The menu has three main courses to choose from.

Pasta bake   Fish and chips   Vegetarian hot pot

The customers at table 1 order one Pasta bake, two Fish and chips and one Vegetarian hot pot. To save time when taking their order, Neil writes this.

$$p + 2f + v$$

Neil does not use a '1' in front of the p or v as he knows that, with no number in front of them, they mean '1p' and '1v'.

At table 2 Neil writes this.

$$3p + 2f + 2v$$

What did the customers order at table 2?

Neil wants to know how many of each dish to order altogether for the two tables.

He writes this.

Table 1	+	Table 2	=	Total
$p + 2f + v$	+	$3p + 2f + 2v$	=	$4p + 4f + 3v$

Table 3 orders $3p + f + 2v$ and Table 4 orders $p + 2f$.

What would Neil write down for the total order for tables 3 and 4?

Neil is using **algebra** and so are you!

33

$p + 2f + 3p + f + 2v$ is an example of an **expression**. An expression can have both numbers and letters.

Each part of an expression is called a **term**. p, $2f$, $3p$, f and $2v$ are all terms.

A number is also a term e.g. $3v + 4$ has two terms.

Expressions can be **simplified**. The expression:
$p + 2f + 3p + f + 2v$ can be simplified by adding the terms together to give $4p + 3f + 2v$.

Terms must have the same letter to collect them together. We can simplify $3p + p$ to give $4p$ but we cannot simplify $3p + 2v$.

When using algebra the number always comes first. e.g. $2f$ not $f2$.

We usually write p not $1p$.

Example 4.1

Simplify the expression

$4e + 5f - e + 3f - 7f$

Collect the e terms: $4e - e = 3e$

Collect the f terms: $5f + 3f - 7f = 8f - 7f = f$

Put the terms back together: $3e + f$

Exercise 4a

1. How many terms are in each of these expressions?

   a $5t + 3u - 5w$

   b $5f - c + 6e - 7$

   c $15y + 9x - 9 - 3z + 2w$

2. Simplify these expressions.

   a $4t + 2t$

   b $5p + p + 3p + 7$

   c $4x + 10x + 3y + 8y$

   d $8a + 4b + 7a + b$

   e $6j + 4k + 3j + 5$

   f $11m + 2m + 5n + m + n$

   g $14d + 2e + 4d + 7e$

   h $3v + v + 5 + 5w$

   i $5h + 2i + 8i + i$

3 Simplify these expressions.

    a $5d - 3d$

    b $6e - 5e$

    c $4f + 5f - 2f + 1$

    d $5p + 3q - 2p + 2q$

    e $4m + 3n - 2m + 2n$

    f $v + 2w + 3v - w$

    g $10a + 8b - 5b$

    h $6g - 5g + 3h - 2h$

    i $12k + 4j - 8k$

    j $7c + 8d - 4c - 3c + d$

Here are some more rules for algebra when multiplying or dividing.

We do not use a × sign in algebra.

$5 \times w$ is written as $5w$ and $a \times b$ is written as ab.

We do not use a ÷ sign in algebra.

We write $\frac{t}{5}$ not $t \div 5$.

The order of the letters is not important when multiplying.

    $ab = ba$ so $ab + ba = ab + ab = 2ab$

Example 4.2

Simplify these expressions.

    a $2 \times 4k$ **b** $15d \div 5$

    c $q \times q$ **d** $2 \times d \times e$

    e $4 \times f + 7 \times f$ **f** $3f \times 7g$

    a $2 \times 4k = 8k$

    b $15d \div 5 = 3d$

    c $q \times q = q^2$

    d $2 \times d \times e = 2de$

    e $4 \times f + 7 \times f = 4f + 7f = 11f$

    f $3f \times 7g = 3 \times 7 \times f \times g = 21fg$

Exercise 4b

Simplify each of these expressions.

1. $4 \times h$
2. $k \times 7$
3. $k \times k$
4. $d \times e$
5. $f \times h \times g$
6. $5 \times n \times n$
7. $5 \times v \times w$
8. $3 \times 2d$
9. $2j \times 5k$
10. $2d \times 5d$
11. $12s \div 3$
12. $20p \div 4$
13. $\frac{18t}{6}$
14. $\frac{2t}{4}$
15. $\frac{6s^2}{s}$
16. $3 \times f + 5 \times f$
17. $2 \times a \times b + b \times a$
18. $p \times p + 6p \times p$

Discussion 4.2

Emma and Gary are playing 'Guess the number'.

Emma thinks of a number. She says 'When I add 6 to my number, I get 9'.

What number did Emma think of?

We could write Emma's puzzle as an **equation**.

$$x + 6 = 9$$

x stands for the unknown number.

An equation always has an = sign; an expression does not.

When we find the unknown number, we have solved the equation. For Emma's puzzle,

$$x = 3$$

Gary thinks of a number. He calls it g.

He says 'When I multiply my number by 4, I get 20'.

We can write this as an equation.

$$4g = 20$$

Can you solve this equation to find Gary's number?

Make up a 'guess the number question' and ask other pupils in the class to solve it.

Example 4.3

Solve this equation. $x + 2 = 9$

We started with x and added 2 to get 9. The inverse of $+2$ is -2 so we need to subtract 2 from both sides of the equation.

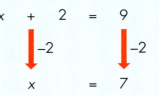

Exercise 4c

Solve these equations. Set your work out as shown in Example 4.3.

1. $t + 7 = 13$
2. $5t = 35$
3. $4j = 32$
4. $d + 4 = 9$
5. $h - 7 = 19$
6. $10m = 100$
7. $q - 1 = 12$
8. $11g = 11$
9. $6d = 24$
10. $19 - v = 12$

Discussion 4.3

In Exercise 4c the questions had only one operation. It is more difficult to solve equations with two operations. Can you make up a question with two operations for other pupils to guess the answer to? Ask another pupil to solve your question. Why is this more difficult to solve?

One way to solve equations with more than one operation is to use function machines.

The equation $4x + 1 = 13$ can be shown by this function machine.

We can solve the equation $4x + 1 = 13$ by finding the inverse of this function machine.

How would you find the inverse of this function machine? Explain the steps in your answer. What is the value of x?

Solve the equation $2h - 1 = 19$

First draw the function machine for the equation.

What is the inverse of this function machine?

What is the value of h?

What do you notice about the order of the operations for the inverse of the function machines?

By first drawing the function machine and finding its inverse solve the equation $3t - 5 = 16$.

Exercise 4d

1. Draw the inverse of these function machines.

   a) x → ×5 → +4 → 14

   b) x → ÷3 → −2 → 5

   c) x → −4 → ÷7 → 4

   d) x → +2 → ×3 → 12

Solve these equations by drawing the function machine first and then the inverse function machine to solve the equation.

2. $4q + 9 = 17$
3. $5g - 6 = 19$
4. $2m - 10 = 30$
5. $8d + 4 = 28$
6. $3p + 5 = 26$
7. $5j - 6 = 24$
8. $3v + 22 = 34$
9. $4k - 1 = 5$
10. $4y - 11 = 23$

Using the function machine takes a lot of time so when you know the correct order to carry out the inverse operations it is easier to set your work out as shown in Example 4.4.

Example 4.4

Solve $5j - 6 = 24$

From using function machines, the inverse operations were used in the opposite order so first do the inverse of −6 which is +6, and then do the inverse of ×5 which is ÷5 to both sides of the equation.

Now check whether your answer is correct by putting it back into the left hand side of the equation.

$5 \times 6 - 6 = 24$

This is the same as the right hand side, so the answer is correct.

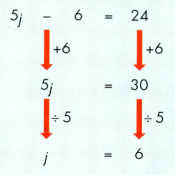

Exercise 4e

Solve these equations using the method in Example 4.4 and check your answers.

1. $4c - 7 = 21$
2. $6y - 4 = 32$
3. $5w + 3 = 28$
4. $4e + 3 = 19$
5. $2g - 11 = 33$
6. $7f + 1 = 57$
7. $3u - 8 = 31$
8. $6t + 6 = 36$
9. $9q + 4 = 67$
10. $8m + 9 = 13$

Activity 4.1

In expressions the number that a letter represents is sometimes known. This can be used to calculate the **value** of an expression. Replacing a letter with a number in an expression is called **substitution**.

Example 4.5

Find the value of these expressions when $k = 4$ and $j = 3$:

a $k + 3 = 4 + 3 = 7$
b $3k = 3 \times 4 = 12$
c $\frac{k}{2} = \frac{4}{2} = 2$
d $k^2 = 4^2 = 16$
e $kj = 4 \times 3 = 12$
f $3k^2j = 3 \times 4^2 \times 3 = 3 \times 16 \times 3 = 144$

Exercise 4f

1. Find the value of these when $t = 2$, $u = 5$, $w = 0$
   a. $6u$
   b. $8t$
   c. $3w$
   d. $3t + 5u$
   e. $4t - u$
   f. u^2
   g. ut
   h. $3ut$
   i. $5t - u + 4$
   j. $6u - 3t + 5w$
   k. $t^2 + u^2 - 10$

2. Substitute these values for d, e and f to find the values of these expressions when $d = 3$, $e = 4$, $f = 1$
   a. $2d$
   b. de
   c. df
   d. $5d + 3e$
   e. e^2
   f. def
   g. $5ed$
   h. $\dfrac{16d}{2}$
   i. $\dfrac{e^2}{f^2}$
   j. $e^2 f^2$
   k. $(2e)^2$

Activity 4.2

Activity 4.3

Consolidation Exercise 1

Chapter 4: Algebra

1 Draw the inverse function machines for these.

a $3 \longrightarrow \boxed{\times 5} \longrightarrow \boxed{-2} \longrightarrow 13$

b $5 \longrightarrow \boxed{\div 5} \longrightarrow \boxed{+7} \longrightarrow 8$

c $t \longrightarrow \boxed{\times 6} \longrightarrow \boxed{-4} \longrightarrow 8$

d $m \longrightarrow \boxed{+7} \longrightarrow \boxed{\div 2} \longrightarrow 5$

2 Solve these equations. Remember to set your work out properly.

Check your solution by putting your answer back into the equation.

a $4d = 24$ **b** $12f = 0$

c $2x - 4 = 10$ **d** $5q - 1 = 14$

e $4f + 7 = 23$ **f** $18 = 2 + 4e$

g $\dfrac{t}{9} = 6$ **h** $\dfrac{20}{k} = 5$

i $3w + 5w = 64$ **j** $4v - 3v + 31 = 42$

k $\dfrac{h}{2} + 3 = 7$ **l** $6q - 42 = 0$

3 Simplify these expressions.

a $10h + h + 6h - 3h$

b $2 \times j$

c $3 \times 2 \times k$

d $4d + 5e - 2e + 6d$

e $g \times g$

f $8n + 5m - n - 2m + 3n$

g $p \times q \times r$

h $9 \times c \times t$

i $u \times 3 \times 2 \times w$

j $3k + 4 - 2k + 7$

k $5h + j + 2 - 3h + 3$

l $5 \times f \times f$

Chapter 4: Algebra

4 Find the value of each expression by substituting the values
$c = 3$, $d = 5$, $e = 2$, $g = 0$, for c, d, e and g.

a $6d$

b $2d - c$

c de

d $4cd$

e $2g + d$

f $2e + 5d$

g deg

h $d^2 + e^2$

i $2d^2 - 2c$

j $c^2 - e^3$

5 Find the value of each expression in the table using these
values: $p = 2$, $q = 3$, $r = 10$, $s = 0$

Then put the letter that matches the value into the grid. When
you have filled the grid you will receive a message about this
chapter.

The first one has been done for you – the value of the
expression is 0, so the letter G goes into the box below any
0's in the grid.

Expression	Value	Letter
$q - 3$	0	G
q^2		A
$5pq$		R
$r - 2q$		L
$8p - 2q$		I
$pqr - qrs$		B
$pq + qr$		E
p^2r		T
$r^2 - q^2 - p^2$		S

9	4	0	36	60	30	9		10	87		0	30	36	9	40
		G									G				

5 3-D Shape

In this chapter I am learning to:
- recognise and name common 3-D shapes and understand their properties
- understand the relationship between 2-D and 3-D shapes
- draw nets of 3-D shapes.

Discussion 5.1

What does 3-D mean? Find some 3-D shapes in the classroom and name them.

What shapes would you find in a supermarket? What shape is a tin of beans? What shape is an orange?

What is meant by the properties of a shape?

In pairs describe and name this shape. Write down at least three properties of the shape.

Activity Sheet 5.1

Activity 5.1

Exercise 5a

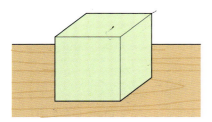

1. This shape sits on a horizontal table. Name the shape.

2. What is the main difference between this shape and a cuboid?

3. How many of the following has the shape
   a edges   b vertices
   c faces   d congruent faces?

4. a How many small cubes make up the larger cube on the left?

   b Each small cube has six faces but not all of these faces are coloured. What is the largest number of coloured faces a small cube has?

   c Copy and complete the table.

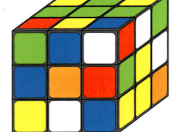

Coloured faces	0	1	2	3	4	5	6
Total number of cubes							

43

d Check that your total number of cubes in part **c** agrees with your answer to part **a**.

5 What is the name for a special cuboid with 12 equal edges?

6 Write down as many uses of cubes in real life that you can think of. Check your list with a friend.

Exercise 5b

1 a On centimetre squared paper rule a set of co-ordinate axes that range from 0 to 10 on both axes.

b Plot and join these points in order (4, 2) (8, 2) (8, 6) (4, 6) (4, 2).

c What shape have you drawn?

d What are the co-ordinates of the mid-point of this shape?

e On the same grid plot and join these points in order (6, 4) (10, 4) (10, 8) (6, 8) (6, 4).

f What is the name of the second shape that you have drawn?

g Is the second shape congruent to the first shape?

h Finally join these points with straight lines: (4, 6) to (6, 8), (4, 2) to (6, 4), (8, 2) to (10, 4), (8, 6) to (10, 8).

i Name the shape you have drawn.

j Mark on a set of four parallel lines.

2 a Draw another set of axes and draw a different sized cube.

b List your co-ordinates and get a friend to check that they produce a cube by plotting them.

3 a Without drawing a co-ordinate grid, draw a 4 cm cube on squared paper.

b Rub out the edges that would be hidden to make your cube look like a closed box.

c Make the closed box look like an empty box without a lid.

4 To draw an accurate full size cube, how many dimensions do you need to know?

5 a Copy this cuboid onto squared paper and label the vertices as shown.

b Which edges are the same length as BC?

c Which edges are parallel to CD?

d Which face is parallel to ABGH?

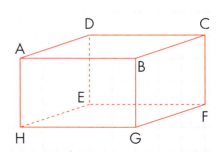

Discussion 5.2

Look at the shape. If this shape was sliced very thinly at right-angles along its length what shape would the slices be? This is called a **cross-section**. If the cross-section is both constant and a polygon the shape is a **prism**. What is this shape called?

Where would you see this shape in real life?

Is a cube a prism? What about a cuboid? What shape is the cross-section of a cuboid? Are these shapes prisms? What are these solids called?

Exercise 5c

i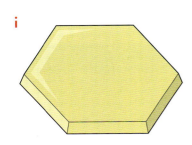

ii

1 Use the triangular prism shown in Discussion 5.2 in this question.

   a How many faces has the prism?

   b What shape are the faces?

   c Are any of the faces congruent?

   d How many **i** edges **ii** vertices has the prism?

2 a The objects on the left are two examples of the same type of prism. What type of prism is this? What assumption are you making about the pencil in **ii** in your answer?

   b How many faces has each of these prisms?

   c What shape are the faces and how many of each shape are there?

   d How many **i** vertices **ii** edges has each prism?

   e If the ends are in the shape of a regular polygon what can you say about the other faces?

   f Where might you find the prism labelled **i**?

3 What shape would a group of stacked 20 pence pieces make?

4 A biscuit manufacturer makes pentagonal shaped biscuits. What shape of container would be suitable to hold pentagonal biscuits without any wasted space?

5 What would a 3-D shape with a constant cross-section of ten sided polygons be called?

6 Part of a cuboid is shown. Copy and complete the diagram on squared paper.

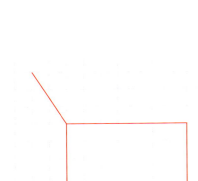

Discussion 5.3

What are these 3-D shapes called? What do all these solids have in common?

a  b 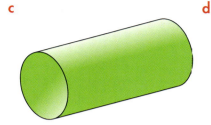 c d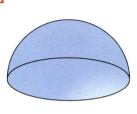

Are these shapes prisms? Explain your answer.

Which of the shapes shown above has a constant cross-section?

Which of the shapes has a circular base and a vertex that is not on the base?

Which figure has all its points equidistant from its centre point?

Activity Sheet 5.2

Activity 5.2

Exercise 5d

1 Copy and complete the table.

Shape	Number of flat (plane) faces	Number of curved surfaces	Number of vertices	Number of straight edges
Sphere				
Cone				
Cylinder				
Hemisphere				

2 What shape would best describe half of a watermelon?

3 A supermarket receives a delivery. Packs of cereal are packed in cardboard boxes and cylindrical tins of baked beans are packed in similar sized cardboard boxes. Which method of packaging is more efficient? Explain your answer.

4 Sketch these on squared paper.

   a sphere   b cone   c cylinder   d hemisphere

Pyramids are named according to their bases. The pyramids shown in **a** are **square pyramids** (also known as **square-based pyramids**). Name the rest of the pyramids according to their bases.

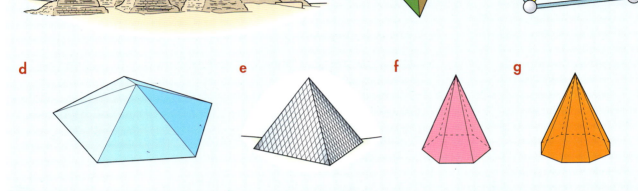

a   b   c
d   e   f   g

Triangular pyramids have a special name. They are known as **tetrahedrons**.

Exercise 5e

1. Is a pyramid a prism? Explain your answer.
2. **a** What type of pyramid is this tea-bag?

  b How many
   i faces
   ii edges
   iii vertices has this pyramid?

3 **a** Copy the square pyramid onto squared paper and label the vertices as shown.

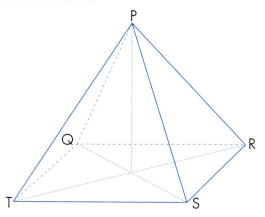

Start by drawing a parallelogram, then mark the centre and move vertically up from the centre to point P. The dashed lines represent hidden edges and the dotted lines are to help locate the centre of the base and the point P directly over the centre.

b The square face that is the base is named QRST. Name the triangular faces that are the sides.

c Are the triangular faces congruent?

d Name three edges equal in length to RS.

e How many edges are equal in length to PT?

4 Here is a sketch of a tetrahedron.

a Copy it onto squared paper.

b How many faces has a tetrahedron?

c How many of these faces are congruent?

d How many edges does it have?

e How many vertices does it have?

f Name the edges that are equal in length to DC.

g A regular tetrahedron is one in which the four triangles are equilateral. Is the tetrahedron ABCD regular?

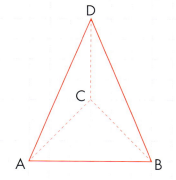

Flat surfaces are called **planes**. Planes are **horizontal, vertical** or **oblique.**

A **polyhedron** is a solid shape with plane faces and straight edges. The plural of polyhedron is **polyhedra**.

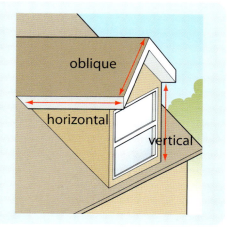

Example 5.1

Name this 3-D shape.

This polyhedron is an octagonal pyramid.

How many horizontal planes has the shape? 1

How many vertical planes has the shape? 0

How many oblique planes has the shape? 8

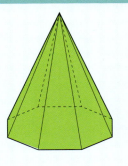

Discussion 5.4

Name a solid shape with two horizontal and four vertical planes only.

Name a prism with two horizontal and six vertical planes.

Name a shape with a single horizontal plane and four oblique planes only.

Is a cylinder a polyhedron? Explain your answer.

Is a hexagonal pyramid a polyhedron? Explain your answer.

Are all prisms and pyramids polyhedra?

A Swiss mathematician, Leonard Euler (1707–83), discovered a formula linking the number of faces, edges and vertices for any polyhedron. See if you can find it too by doing Activity 5.3.

Activity Sheet 5.3

Activity 5.3

Activity Sheet 5.4

Activity 5.4

Isometric dot paper is useful for drawing pictures of 3-D figures. It is important to use the paper the right way up.

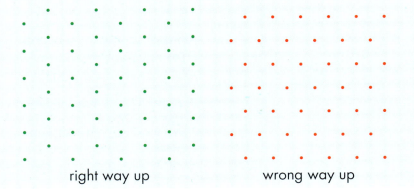

right way up   wrong way up

Exercise 5f

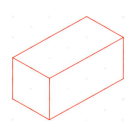

1. Copy this cuboid onto 1 cm isometric paper. Write down its dimensions.

2. **a** Here are parts of several cuboids. Copy and complete them and write down their dimensions.

i    ii    iii    iv

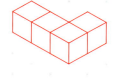

b Which two cuboids are congruent?

3. On isometric paper draw cuboids with these dimensions.

	Height	Width	Length
a	3 cm	3 cm	2 cm
b	4 cm	2 cm	3 cm

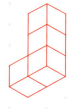

4. Four cubes have been joined together as shown.

   a Are the arrangements different?

   b In pairs, and using multilink cubes to help, arrange four cubes in as many **different** ways as possible. Draw your arrangements on isometric paper.

Activity 5.5

Activity Sheet 5.5

Discussion 5.5

What shape are most boxes? What shape are most pizza and cake boxes? What shape are most pizzas and cakes? Is this an efficient use of packaging?

A pattern or shape which can be folded to make a solid is called a **net**.

Cylindrical boxes could be used for packaging pizzas and cakes to reduce waste. Why do you think cylindrical boxes are not used?

Exercise 5g

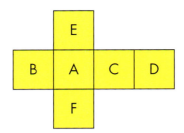

1. The net of a cube is shown.
   a. Copy this net onto squared paper and label the faces as shown, then cut it out.
   b. Fold the net into a cube and stick it together.
   c. If face A is the base, describe the other faces when the cube is constructed.
   d. If face C is the top, describe the other faces when the cube is constructed.

2. a. Draw an accurate net for a 2 cm cube on squared paper.
   b. Cut out your net and check it folds to make a 2 cm cube.

3. There is more than one net of a cube. Another example is shown.

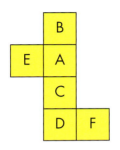

   a. Copy the net, label the faces, cut it out and check that it folds up into a cube.
   b. If face A is the base describe the other faces.
   c. Work with a partner and draw as many different nets of a cube as you can. Remember that rotations and reflections count as the same net.

4. a. A die has six faces. What do you notice about the three pairs of opposite faces?
   b. Copy and complete each of these nets of a die in two different ways.

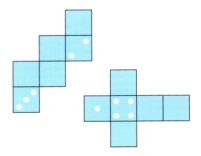

5. Which is the correct cube for the net shown?

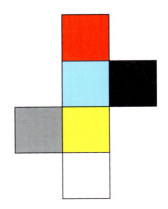

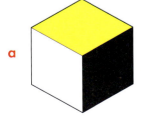 a   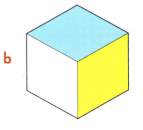 b   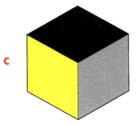 c

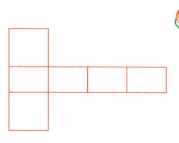

6 This net, drawn on centimetre squared paper, will fold up to make a cuboid.

   a What are the dimensions of this cuboid?

   b Sketch at least two different nets for this cuboid.

7 Draw accurate nets for a cuboid with these dimensions.

   a Length 5 cm, Breadth 2 cm, Height 2 cm

   b Length 3 cm, Breadth 1 cm, Height 4 cm

8 Sketch nets for these solids.

   a triangular prism   b square pyramid   c cylinder

Activity 5.6

Activity 5.7

Consolidation Exercise 1

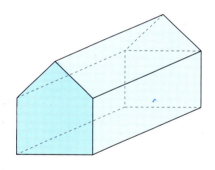

1 a Where would you commonly see this shape?

  b What is the name of this shape?

  c How many faces has this shape?

  d What shape are the faces and how many are there of each shape?

  e Which faces would you expect to be congruent?

  f How many i vertices ii edges has this shape?

  g The shape can also be split into which other two prisms?

  h Would you expect the total faces, edges and vertices of the two prisms to equal the answers in parts c and f? Explain your answer.

2 Copy these prisms onto squared paper. Name each prism.

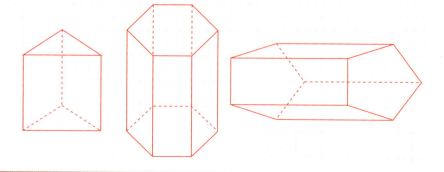

Decimals

In this chapter, I am learning to:
- multiply decimal numbers up to three decimal places
- round answers to one or two decimal places
- use estimation
- divide decimal numbers by whole numbers and give answers to two decimal places.

You can round numbers to the **nearest whole number**.

The digit in the tenths place tells us whether or not to go up to the next whole number.

Remember – when rounding to the nearest whole number, if the tenths digit is 5 or more then go up to the next whole number.

6.<mark>7</mark> rounds to 7 14.<mark>3</mark>2 rounds to 14

659.<mark>7</mark>123 rounds to 660 38.<mark>5</mark>3 rounds to 39

Exercise 6a

Round these to **a** the nearest whole number **b** the nearest 10

1 23.4
2 76.76
3 1.71
4 1258.89
5 39.6
6 564.2999
7 0.3276
8 299.6341
9 80.47
10 101.4999

Discussion 6.1

Paul says that 33.3 multiplied by 8 is 234.4. Does this seem sensible? How do you know?

Peter says that 77.8 times 92 is 715.76. Is he right?

Before multiplying large numbers or decimal numbers it is always a good idea to estimate first.

What would be a sensible estimate for 28 times 3.9? What about 1850 times 11.23? When estimating we usually round numbers in the thousands to the nearest thousand. What should a number in the hundreds be rounded to? A number in the tens? A decimal number less than 10?

Estimate 3.5 × 12.7 × 48.7

Example 6.1

Estimate the answer to 42.7 times 8, then use multiplication to find the exact answer.

Estimate as 40 times 8 = 320

$$\begin{array}{r} ^{2}4^{5}2.7 \\ \times\ 8 \\ \hline 3\ 4\ 1.6 \end{array}$$

Exercise 6b

Estimate the answers to these.

1   28 × 11.1
2   45.6 × 54.3
3   312 × 21.9
4   2877 × 6.3
5   1.82 × 650
6   773 × 78.9
7   54 × 17.8
8   9.91 × 8650
9   7.6 × 23.9 × 187.2
10   2.5 × 32.5 × 61.7
11   63.7 × 5
12   123 × 7.5
13   16.8 × 23
14   48.04 × 77
15   777 × 15.9

Now use long multiplication to find the exact answers for Questions **11–15**.

Exercise 6c

1. The circumference of a circle is approximately 3.14 times its diameter. What is the circumference of a circle of diameter 12 cm?

2. What is the area of a rectangle measuring 67.9 cm by 82 cm?

3. A packet of frozen prawns weighs 1.45 kg. How much would eight of these packets weigh in total?

4. A DVD case is 1.45 cm wide. If 28 of these are stacked next to each other on a shelf, what length of shelf is used?

5. Sam bought 28 tins of cat food costing £0.69 each. How much did the tins cost in total?

6. Rod buys 8 square metres of carpet costing £23.99 per square metre. How much does he spend?

7. Rebecca earns the minimum wage of £5.52 per hour. How much does she earn if she works a 37-hour week?

8. a 33 times 15 = 495. What is 3.3 times 15?
   b 28 × £12.75 = £357. What is 28 × £127.50?
   c 2.8 × 32.5 × 12.5 = 1137.5. What is 28 × 3.25 × 1.25?

Discussion 6.2

Florence Griffith Joyner holds the world record for the 100 metres. She ran it in a time of 10.49 seconds on 16th July 1988 at Indianapolis, USA. What was her time rounded to the nearest whole number?

What was her time rounded to one decimal place?

Jason measures the width of a window as 1.246 metres. What is this length rounded to one decimal place?

Conor and Neil are both 155 cm tall. Conor insists he is taller than Neil. Can Conor be right?

Conor and Neil had a race over a mile and both boys recorded times of 5 minutes and 8 seconds but Neil insists he won the race. How is this possible?

Albert divides 22 by 8 using his calculator and gets 2.75. How many decimal places are in this answer? Albert needs to round his answer to one decimal place. He isn't sure whether the answer is 2.7 or 2.8. Why is Albert confused? What rule should Albert use to round the answer to one decimal place? What is 2.75 rounded to one decimal place?

When rounding numbers to **one decimal place** the digit in the hundredths place tells us whether to increase the tenths digit or not. If the digit in the hundredths place is 5 or more, then increase the tenths digit by one, otherwise the tenths digit does not change.

2.6 8 rounds to 2.7 to one decimal place.

214.7 1 56 rounds to 214.7 to one decimal place.

0.3 5 412 rounds to 0.4 to one decimal place

563.9 6 25 rounds to 564.0 (not just 564)

0.9 7 5 rounds to 1.0

The hundredths digit in 0.975 is 7. Since it is five or more we add 1 to the digit in the tenths place, 9, to get 10. However, we have to carry the 1 across to the units column and add to get 1. So our answer is 1.0. Note this answer should not be further rounded to 1!

```
U  .  t    h  th
0  .  9⁺¹ (7) 5
1  .  0
```

round up
(9 tenths + 1 tenth
= 10 tenths = 1.0)

Exercise 6d

1 Round these numbers to one decimal place.

- **a** 6.49
- **b** 0.777
- **c** 1.25
- **d** 88.04
- **e** 12.31
- **f** 234.92
- **g** 100.97
- **h** 0.053
- **i** 1.032
- **j** 123.456
- **k** 19.9999

2 Give your answer to these to one decimal place.

- **a** 74.73×9.1
- **b** $293 \div 11$
- **c** $4010 \div 9$
- **d** 7.5863×7
- **e** $48 \div 7$
- **f** 3.45^2
- **g** 23.82^3
- **h** $\sqrt{14}$
- **i** $4 \div 7 + 7 \div 4$
- **j** $(6.32 + 2.99) \div 0.47$
- **k** $4.808^2 - 1.32^3$

3 Linford ran 100 m in 10.25 seconds and came first. Carl came third in 10.32 seconds.

- **a** Round both times to one decimal place.
- **b** Maurice came second. What time could he have run? Whatever time he ran, what must it be to one decimal place?

4 A pound (lb) is 0.454 kg.

    a How many kilograms would 200 lb be equivalent to?

    b Round 0.454 kg to one decimal place and use your answer to find the weight of 200 lb in kilograms.

    c What is the difference between these answers for 200 lb? Comment on your answer.

5 Barry measures the width of the space between two cupboards as 0.7 metres. Could a fridge 0.72 m wide fit in this space? Explain your answer.

6 a Multiply 1.27 by 2.38 and divide your answer by 3.42. Write down your answer to one decimal place.

    b Round 1.27 and 2.38 to one decimal place and find their product. Round 3.42 to one decimal place and divide this into the product. What is your answer to one decimal place?

    c Has rounding to one decimal place made any difference to the answer you got in part **a**?

    d Is this always going to be the case? Work with a partner and choose three decimal numbers, to at least two decimal places, to either prove or disprove your answer.

Activity Sheet 6.1

Activity 6.1

Discussion 6.3

It is sometimes necessary to round numbers to two decimal places. Can you think of any situations where this would be necessary? Why would it be necessary to round to two decimal places instead of one decimal place?

Lisa and Deborah both ran 100 m in 15.1 seconds. Lisa won. How is this possible? When would it be sensible to give answers to one decimal place? What measurements in everyday life are given to one decimal place? What about two decimal places? What are the rules of rounding to one decimal place? What do you think the rules would be when rounding to two decimal places?

Exercise 6e

1. Round these numbers to two decimal places.

   a 3.462
   b 387.744
   c 2.458
   d 5.815
   e 32.477
   f 297.399
   g 2.3096
   h 10.001
   i 0.008
   j 0.0989

2. a Write down at least two different numbers that round to 2.5 when rounded to one decimal place.

   b Write down at least two different numbers that round to 2.00 when rounded to two decimal places.

   c What is the smallest number which will round to 12.2 to one decimal place?

   d What is the largest number which will round to 12.2 to one decimal place?

   e What is the smallest number which will round to 1.78 to two decimal places?

   f What is the largest number which will round to 1.78 to two decimal places?

3. Give your answer to these to two decimal places.

   a 18.43×1.33
   b $58 \div 23$
   c $9.37 \div 0.28$
   d 183×0.076
   e $12.7 \div 7$
   f 6.94^2
   g 14.88^3
   h $\sqrt{81.7}$

4. Give your answer to these to two decimal places.

   a $2.3 + 6.2 \times 0.72$
   b $(2.3 + 6.2) \times 0.72$
   c $7^2 - \frac{1}{5} \times 28.04$
   d $2.44 \times \sqrt{7} \times 9$

Activity Sheet 6.2

Activity 6.2

Example 6.2

Mervyn bought eight identical tins of paint. The total cost was £98.56. How much did each tin cost?

First it is useful to have an idea of the answer by estimating.

£98.56 is approximately 100

To divide 100 by 8 I can divide 100 by 4 and then by 2, i.e.
100 ÷ 4 = 25 and 25 ÷ 2 = 12.5

Estimate is £12.50

Now use division to calculate the exact answer.

$$8 \overline{\smash{)}£\ 9\ ^{1}8\ .\ ^{2}5\ ^{1}6}$$
$$\phantom{8\overline{\smash{)}}}£\ 1\ 2\ .\ 3\ 2$$

Exercise 6f

1. Share £86.85 equally between three friends.

2. Five identical new laptops cost £2629.95. How much does each laptop cost?

3. Six identical empty jars weigh a total of 378.48 g. What is the weight of one empty jar?

4. Steve threw his javelin a total of 769.23 m in nine practice throws. What was the average distance he threw?

5. Seven dominoes are laid end to end and their combined length is measured. If the total length is 31.22 cm, what is the length of each domino?

Discussion 6.4

Fifteen inches is 38.1 cm. How can I find out how centimetres are in one inch?

Without using long division (or a calculator) how could a number be divided by 18? What about dividing a number by 17 or 29? What is different about the numbers in these two cases?

Exercise 6g

1. Sixteen one euro coins stacked on top of each other measure 37.28 mm high. What is the thickness of a one euro coin?

2. A class of 25 pupils raised a grand total of £711.75 during a sponsored silence. How much did each pupil raise on average?

3. Twenty-eight litres of diesel cost Roger £29.96. How much does each litre cost?

4. £24 is worth 40.56 euro. How many euro is £1 worth?

5. Thirteen members of a lottery syndicate share £6 833 087.04 equally. How much do they each receive?

6. Exactly 46 DVDs fit on a shelf. If the shelf measures 682.64 mm in length, what width is a DVD case?

7. The product of two numbers is 22.62. If one of the numbers is 87, what is the other?

Activity Sheet 6.3

Activity 6.3

Discussion 6.5

What is $\frac{1}{3}$ of 60?

$\frac{1}{3}$ as a decimal is 0.33333 ... What is $\frac{1}{3}$ as a decimal to three decimal places? Multiply this answer by 60.

Why is this answer different to the first one?

You must be careful when rounding not to introduce error unnecessarily.

Make a sensible estimate for 0.454×28

Money is recorded to two decimal places, so why might someone earn £7.253 per hour?

Example 6.3

Find the product of 62.305 and 24.

Estimate first.

$60 \times 20 = 1200$

Now just multiply as you did earlier with numbers to two decimal places.

```
   6 2 . 3 0 5     total
 ×       2 4      number
 ─────────────    of decimal
   2 4 9 2 2 0    places is 3
 1 2 4 6 1 0 0
 ─────────────
 1 4 9 5 . 3 2 0
```

move three places in from the right

Example 6.4

Find the product of 21.65 and 8.6

Estimate first.

20 × 9 = 180

Multiply the numbers just as if they were whole numbers.

```
    ₁²³₅¹.⁴₆ ⁵     total
  ×      8.6      number
  ─────────────   of decimal
     1 2 9 9 0    places is 3
   1 7 3₁2 0 0
  ─────────────
     1 8 6.1 9 0
```

move three places in from the right

Line up the numbers on the right – there is no need to line up the decimal points.

Starting on the right, multiply each digit in the top number by each digit in the bottom number, just as with whole numbers.

Add the products.

Place the decimal point in the answer by starting at the right and moving to the left by the total number of decimal places in the numbers being multiplied.

Check the answer is sensible by comparing with the estimate. 186.190 is close to 180.

Exercise 6h

1. May works a 37-hour week and earns £7.195 an hour.
   a. Estimate May's weekly wage.
   b. Find her weekly wage correct to the nearest penny.

2. Eamon bought 1150 litres of home heating oil at 31.469p per litre. What was his bill? Give your answer in pounds to a sensible degree of accuracy.

3. Penelope fills her car with 60.2 litres of fuel, costing 107.9p per litre.
   a. Her car travels 8.74 km per litre of fuel. How far can she travel before refuelling?
   b. How much did she pay for her fuel?

4. Mr Darling pays his secretary £9.13 per hour.
   a. How much does the secretary earn for a 37.5-hour week?
   b. How much is this over the course of a year (52 weeks)?
   c. Repeat parts a and b with an hourly rate of £9.137
   d. How much extra would this slight increase earn the secretary in one year?

Consolidation Exercise 1

1 Round these numbers to one decimal place.
   a 3.32
   b 76.362
   c 121.25
   d 0.77
   e 5631.823
   f 25.95
   g 88.893
   h 29.99999
   i 489732.01
   j 0.0512

2 What is the product of these?
   a 0.08 and 1.4
   b 0.38 and 0.3
   c 148 and 0.525

3 Round these numbers to two decimal places.
   a 10.871
   b 230.049
   c 6.814711
   d 0.3942
   e 5.1439999
   f 27.636
   g 89.96512
   h 99.995
   i 0.0396
   j 0.0013

4 Give your answer to these to the nearest whole number.
   a 7.9×5.2
   b $14.6 \div 8$
   c $2000 \div 19$
   d 4.328×7
   e $29 \div 3$
   f 1.9^2
   g 1.55^3
   h $4 \div 17 + 17 \div 4$

5 Give your answers to these to one decimal place.
   a 6.25×3.08
   b $1.087 \div 2.44$
   c 1.02^3

6 Give your answers to these to two decimal places.
   a $\sqrt{7}$
   b $0.08 \div \sqrt{0.58}$
   c 293.48×0.799
   d $10.075 \div 3.333^3$

7 A pint is 0.568 litres. How many litres is 85 pints?

8 A nautical league is equivalent to 5.556 km. Elle is a competitor in the Barcelona World Race. She must sail her yacht 7260 nautical leagues around the world. How many kilometres does she sail?

9 Sebastian jogs six miles every morning. A mile is 1609.344 metres. How many metres does he jog in a week? How many kilometres is this?

7 Ratio and Proportion

In this chapter, I am learning to:
- understand and use ratio
- simplify ratios
- understand proportion.

Discussion 7.1

Susan is making a necklace with red and white beads. She arranges them in this pattern.

How many beads are there altogether?

How many of the beads are red?

How many of the beads are white?

Read these statements about the pattern.

$\frac{10}{25}$ of the beads are white.

$\frac{15}{25}$ of the beads are red.

For every three red beads, there are two white beads.

$\frac{2}{5}$ of the beads are white.

$\frac{3}{5}$ of the beads are red.

Which of these statements are true?

Read the last three statements again. Instead of writing these, we can use **ratio** to describe the relationship between red and white beads.

The ratio of white beads to red beads is 2 : 3

What is the ratio of red beads to white beads?

Exercise 7a

1. Jason is planting blue and pink flowers in a window box. He arranges them as shown.

   a Copy and complete these statements.

   There are _____ flowers in the window box.

   _____ of them are blue.

   _____ of them are pink.

   The ratio of pink flowers to blue flowers is _____ : _____

   The ratio of blue flowers to pink flowers is _____ : _____

   For every _____ pink flowers, there are _____ blue flowers.

   b What fraction of the flowers are pink?

   c What fraction of the flowers are blue?

2. A picture in a child's book is shown.

   a Copy and complete these statements.

   There are _____ animals in the picture.

   _____ of them are puppies.

   _____ of them are kittens.

   The ratio of puppies to kittens is _____ : _____

   The ratio of kittens to puppies is _____ : _____

   For every _____ puppies, there are _____ kittens.

   b What fraction of the animals are puppies?

   c What fraction of the animals are kittens?

3. In a snooker tournament there are 32 players. Four of the players are left handed.

   a What is the ratio of left handed players to right handed players?

   b What is the ratio of right handed players to left handed players?

   c What fraction of the players are left handed?

   d What fraction of the players are right handed?

   e Complete this sentence.

   For every left handed player there are ____ right handed players.

Discussion 7.2

What do you think simplifying a ratio means? How could you simplify these ratios?

35 : 50   4 m : 80 cm   0.5 : 7

When a ratio can be simplified so that one of the numbers is a 1, we call this a **unitary ratio.** Write each of the ratios above as a unitary ratio in the form 1 : n.

A unitary ratio may also be written as n : 1. Write each of the ratios above in the form n : 1.

Does simplifying a ratio and writing a ratio as a unitary ratio mean the same? Explain your answer.

Ratios must be in the same units before they are simplified.

Example 7.1

Simplify 3 kg : 500 g

We must change 3 kg to 3000 kg before we can simplify this ratio.

Once both numbers in a ratio are expressed in the same units, you do not need to write the units after the number.

3 kg : 500 g = 3000 : 500 = 6 : 1 (by dividing both sides of the ratio by 500).

Simplified ratios should not have fraction or decimals.

Exercise 7b

1   Simplify these ratios.
    a 8 : 4   b 15 : 25
    c 35 : 7   d 18 : 24
    e 20 : 32   f 12 : 9
    g 42 : 28   h 40 : 16
    i 4 : 14   j 300 : 400

2   Copy and complete.
    a 16 : ? = 4 : 1   b 3 : 15 = 9 : ?
    c 50 : ? = 200 : 80   d 21 : 33 = 14 : ?
    e ? : 12 = 12 : 36

3 Write each of the ratios as unitary ratios, in the form 1 : n. Round answers to one decimal place, if required.

   a 3 : 12   b 10 : 20
   c 18 : 24   d 17 : 51
   e 42 : 21

4 Simplify these ratios.

   a 80 cm : 4 m   b £5 : 50p
   c 2 litres : 200 ml   d 35p : £1
   e 20 mm : 4 cm   f 6 m : 20 cm
   g £4.25 : £12.50   h 700 m : 0.5 km

In Questions 5–7 simplify the ratios in your answers, where possible.

5 In a Youth Group, there are 22 girls and 18 boys.

   a What is the ratio of girls to boys?
   b What is the ratio of boys to girls?

6 To plant his seedlings, Geoff uses 15 kg of soil and 10 kg of compost.

   a What is the ratio of soil to compost?
   b What is the ratio of compost to soil?

7 During a sponsored swim, Angela gets £1.20 per length and Andrew gets 95p per length. Write down and simplify the ratio of the amount Angela gets per length to the amount Andrew gets per length.

Activity Sheet 7.1

Activity 7.1

Discussion 7.3

To make an orange drink, you need to use orange squash and water in the ratio 8 : 1

How else could you give this information?

Sophie pours 40 ml of squash into a jug. How much water does she need to add to make the drink? How much of the drink will this make?

Craig pours 240 ml of water into a jug. How much orange squash does he need to add to make the drink? How much of the drink will this make?

Carol has made up 450 ml of the drink.

How much squash did she use?

How much water did she use?

Exercise 7c

1. To make a blackcurrant drink you need to use blackcurrant cordial and water in the ratio 1 : 6

   a Matt pours 30 ml of cordial into a glass.
      i How much water does he need to add to make the drink?
      ii How much of the drink does this make?

   b Marie pours 120 ml of water into a glass.
      i How much cordial does she need to add to make the drink?
      ii How much of the drink does this make?

   c Michael made up 350 ml of the drink.
      i How much cordial did he use?
      ii How much water did he use?

2. A bag of beads contains black and white beads in the ratio 5 : 2

   There are six white beads in the bag.

   a How many black beads are there?
   b How many beads are in the bag altogether?

3. To plant his cuttings, Ned uses a mixture of sand and compost in the ratio 3 : 10

   a If he uses 2 kg of compost, how much sand will he need?
   b If he uses 1.5 kg of sand, how much compost will he need?
   c Ned has made up 5.2 kg of the mixture.
      i How much sand has he used?
      ii How much compost has he used?

4. To provide a suitable meadow for horses to graze on, a mixture of paddock grass seeds and herb seeds is sown. The ratio of grass seeds to herb seeds is 14 : 1

   a If 3 kg of herb seeds is used, what weight of paddock grass seeds will be needed?
   b If 60 kg of the mixture is used, what weight of herb seeds was used?
   c What weight of paddock grass seeds was used in **b**?

5 Different amounts and colours of purple paint are made by mixing red and blue paint as shown in the table.

Colour name	Moroccan Sunset	Garnet	Amethyst	Purple Haze	Damson
Ratio of blue paint to red paint	1 : 2	1 : 3	2 : 5	3 : 8	
Amount of blue paint (ml)	300	200			420
Amount of red paint (ml)	600		5400		320
Amount of purple paint (ml)	900			2200	

Copy and complete the table. The first one has been done for you.

Example 7.2

Seven pencils cost £2.45. Find the cost of 18 pencils.

To find the answer, first find the cost of one pencil and then multiply by 18

Set your work out like this.

Seven pencils   £2.45

One pencil   £2.45 ÷ 7 = £0.35

18 pencils   £0.35 × 18 = £6.30

To answer this question we are using **proportion**.

Exercise 7d

Show all your working out in this exercise.

1 A recipe for four people uses 800 g of beef. How much beef would be needed for six people?

2 Robyn spent £20.97 on three identical cushions. How much would five of the same cushions cost?

3 Eight apples cost £2.56. What would you pay for six of the same apples?

4 The ingredients for banana and walnut loaf are shown.

> 350 g mashed banana
> 175 g walnut pieces
> 110 g plain flour
> 110 g wholemeal flour
> 110 g butter
> 150 g soft brown sugar
> 1 teaspoon baking powder
> 1 teaspoon cinnamon
> grated zest of lemon or orange
> Serves 10 people.

Write down the ingredients needed for 15 people.

5. A catering company keeps a record of how much of each type of food is needed for different numbers of guests.

   Copy and complete the table for the amounts of chicken, broccoli, potatoes and gravy needed for 60, 80 and 120 guests.

	60 guests	80 guests	120 guests
Chicken (kg)	10.8		
Broccoli (kg)			14.4
Potatoes (kg)		20	
Gravy (litres)		6.3	

Activity 7.2

Consolidation Exercise 1

1. Write each of these ratios in its simplest form.
   a 6 : 8
   b 15 : 33
   c 42 : 36
   d 25 : 200
   e 27 : 18
   f 30 : 300
   g 16 : 6
   h 40 : 16
   i 38 : 8
   j 50 : 125

2. One of the three ratios is not the same as the other two. Pick the odd one out each time.
   a 3 : 5   15 : 20   9 : 15
   b 4 : 1   16 : 64   100 : 25
   c 15 : 50   45 : 100   6 : 20
   d 8 : 9   4 : 3   16 : 12

3. Five highlighter pens cost £7.25. Find the cost of:
   a eight highlighter pens
   b 30 highlighter pens.

4. In a class there are 16 boys and 12 girls.
   a What is the ratio of boys to girls? Give your answer in its simplest form.
   b What is the ratio of girls to boys? Give your answer in its simplest form.

In the year group, the ratio of boys to girls is the same as in this class. There are 196 pupils in the year group.

   c How many boys are there?

   d How many girls are there?

5 Simplify these ratios.

   a 70 cm : 6 m   **b** £3 : 60p

   c 8 : 2.5   **d** 8 cm : 120 mm

   e 420 g : 6 kg

6 Alex is making a bracelet with blue and white beads. He uses two white beads for every three blue beads.

Alex uses 30 beads altogether.

   a How many white beads does he use?

   b How many blue beads does he use?

7 Gary is arranging flowers for a wedding reception. He has purple and white flowers and a number of different sized vases.

He wants to arrange the purple and white flowers in the ratio 5 : 3

Gary puts ten purple flowers into a vase.

   a How many white flowers should he put into the vase?

   b How many flowers will be in the vase altogether?

Gary now chooses a vase that holds 32 flowers.

   c How many purple flowers should he put in the vase?

   d How many white flowers should he put in the vase?

8 Patterns and Sequences

In this chapter, I am learning to:
- describe patterns in sequences
- state rules for sequences in words and using algebra
- use formulae.

Discussion 8.1

Look at the number pattern.

1,   3,   7,   13,   21, ...

A number pattern like this is often called a **sequence**.

Each number in the sequence is called a **term**.

The dots tell us that the sequence continues.

We can work out more terms of the sequence by looking at the **difference** between the terms.

To find the next term in our sequence, we need to add 10. The next term is 31.

What is the term after 31?

What is the one after that?

We can write a **rule** for finding the next term of a sequence. The rule for finding the next term for this sequence is

'add 2 to the difference each time'.

Exercise 8a

a Find the missing number in these sequences.

b Write a rule for finding the next term for each of the sequences.

1	2	5	8	___	___	___
2	125	100	75	50	___	___
3	1	4	9	16	___	___
4	16	8	4	2	___	___
5	3	6	12	24	___	___
6	1	3	6	10	___	___
7	1.8	1.6	1.4	1.2	___	___
8	2	3	5	8	___	___
9	300	30	3	0.3	___	___
10	1000	999	997	994	___	___

Discussion 8.2

Jody is making squares with matchsticks.

1 square
4 matchsticks

2 squares
7 matchsticks

3 squares
10 matchsticks

4 squares
13 matchsticks

She draws a table to show how many matchsticks she has to use to make different numbers of squares.

Number of squares	1	2	3	4
Number of matchsticks	4	7		

What numbers should Jody put in the empty boxes in the table?

How many matchsticks would Jody need to make five squares?

How many matchsticks would Jody need to make eight squares?

How many matchsticks would Jody need to make 100 squares?

We do not want to have to count on to find the answer for 100 squares!

A function machine can be used to help find a rule or **formula** connecting the number of matchsticks and the number of squares.

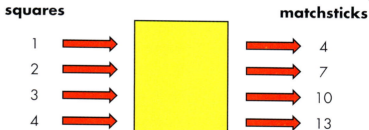

What rule should go in the box?

The difference in the sequence can help to find the rule.

There is a difference of three in the number of matchsticks each time. This tells us that the rule starts with × 3.

$1 \times 3 = 3$

What do we need to do now to get 4?

Will doing the same thing to $2 \times 3 = 6$ get 7?

The rule, in words, to connect the number of matchsticks and the number of squares is:

number of matchsticks = 3 × number of squares + 1

This rule can be written using algebra with m = number of matchsticks and s = number of squares.

$m = 3s + 1$

Exercise 8b

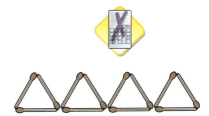

1. Tom is making triangles with matchsticks.

   a Copy and complete the table.

Number of triangles (t)	1	2	3	4
Number of matchsticks (m)				

   b The number of matchsticks forms a sequence. What is the difference for this sequence?

   c Copy and complete the rule connecting the number of triangles and the number of matchsticks in words.

   Number of matchsticks = _____

   d Write your rule using algebra by copying and completing this.

   $m = $ _____

2. Anna is making hexagons using matchsticks.

   a Copy and complete the table.

Number of hexagons (h)	1	2	3	4
Number of matchsticks (m)				

   b The number of matchsticks forms a sequence. What is the difference for this sequence?

   c Copy and complete the rule connecting the number of hexagons and the number of matchsticks in words.

   Number of matchsticks = _____

   d Write your rule using algebra by copying and completing this.

   $m = $ _____

3 Adam is making patterns using matchsticks.

Pattern 1   Pattern 2   Pattern 3

a Copy and complete the table

Pattern (p)	1	2	3	4
Number of matchsticks (m)				

b The number of matchsticks forms a sequence. What is the difference for this sequence?

c Copy and complete the rule connecting the pattern number and the number of matchsticks in words.

Number of matchsticks = _____ × pattern number + _____

d Write your rule using algebra by copying and completing this.

$m = $ _____ + _____

4 Adam makes another pattern.

Pattern 1   Pattern 2   Pattern 3

  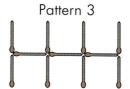

a Copy and complete the table.

Pattern (p)	1	2	3	4
Number of matchsticks (m)				

b The number of matchsticks forms a sequence. What is the difference for this sequence?

c Write a rule connecting pattern number and the number of matchsticks in words.

d Write your rule using algebra.

5 Maureen is making L-shapes with square tiles.

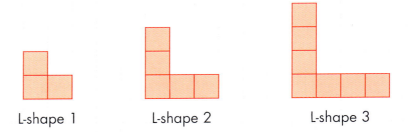

L-shape 1   L-shape 2   L-shape 3

a Copy and complete the table.

L-shape (*n*)	1	2	3	4
Number of tiles (*t*)				

b Write a rule connecting the L-shape and the number of tiles in words.

c Write your rule using algebra.

d How many tiles would Maureen need for L-shape 15?

Activity Sheet 8.1

Activity 8.1

Example 8.1

Darren is cooking chicken that weighs 3 pounds. He uses the **formula**

$$T = 20w + 25$$

where T = time in minutes w = weight of chicken in pounds

to work out how many minutes it will take to cook the chicken.

To work out how long to cook a chicken weighing 3 pounds, use $w = 3$ in the formula.

$T = 20 \times 3 + 25$ (remember that $20w$ means $20 \times w$)

$T = 85$ minutes

Instructions given in algebra are called **formulae**.

Exercise 8c

1. Ryan paints bowls in a china factory. He is paid £200 per week plus £2 for every bowl he paints. He can work out how much he will be paid using the formula:

   $P = 200 + 2b$

   where P = Ryan's pay b = number of bowls

   a One week Ryan painted 45 bowls. How much did he earn that week?
   b The next week, Ryan painted 53 bowls. How much did he earn that week?

2. Eddie repairs electrical appliances. He charges £50 for each call out and then £8 per hour. Eddie can use the formula below to work out how much to charge for each repair.

   $C = 8h + 50$

   where C = charge for repair in £s
   h = number of hours taken

   a Use the formula to work out how much Eddie will charge for repairing a washing machine if it takes him 3 hours.
   b Eddie repairs a fridge freezer. It takes him $2\frac{1}{2}$ hours. How much should he charge the customer?

3. Quik Taxis charge £2.50 plus 40p per mile for each journey.

   The formula, $C = 0.4m + £2.50$,
   where C = cost of taxi
   m = number of miles
   can be used for working out the cost of a taxi for any length of journey.

   a Work out the cost for a five-mile journey.
   b Kieran took a Quik Taxi home, a distance of 7 miles. He gave the driver a £2 tip. What did he pay altogether?

4. Ricky's internet bill is made up of £9 per month plus 1 penny for each minute spent on line. The following formula can be used for working out Ricky's monthly bill.

   $B = 9 + 0.01m$
   where B = monthly bill (£s)
   m = number of minutes spent on line

   a In April, Ricky spent 982 minutes on line. Use the formula to calculate Ricky's bill for April.
   b In May, Ricky spent 43 hours and 34 minutes on line. Use the formula to calculate his bill for May.

5. To print leaflets, Printworks charges £32 plus 3p for each leaflet.
   The formula
   $C = 32 + 0.03n$ can be used for working out the cost of printing any number of leaflets,
   where C = cost of printing (£s) and
   n = number of leaflets.

   a Use the formula to find the cost of printing 3000 leaflets.
   b Find the cost of printing 10 000 leaflets.

Example 8.2

Sometimes we have to use more than one value in a formula.

The formula $s = \dfrac{d}{t}$ is used to work out speed when you know distance and time.

s = speed (metres per second)   d = distance (metres)
t = time (seconds)

Find s when d = 20 metres and t = 5 seconds.

$s = \dfrac{20}{5} = 4$ metres per second (remember that $\dfrac{20}{5}$ means 20 ÷ 5)

Exercise 8d

1 The formula for the volume of a cuboid is

   V = lwh

   where V = volume   l = length   w = width   h = height.

   Use this formula to find V when

   a l = 10 cm   w = 8 cm   h = 12 cm
   b l = 1.8 m   w = 0.7 m   h = 0.6 m
   c l = 128 cm   w = 56 cm   h = 63 cm

2 The formula for the area of a triangle is $A = \tfrac{1}{2}bh$ where

   A = area   b = length of the base of the triangle

   and h = perpendicular height of the triangle

   Use this formula to find the area of these triangles.

   a b = 16 cm   h = 20 cm
   b b = 7.6 cm   h = 9.6 cm
   c b = 1.3 m   h = 0.8 m

3 Use the formula   v = u + at

   to find the value of v when

   a u = 4   a = 10   t = 2
   b u = 2.5   a = 9.8   t = 5
   c u = 0   a = 14.8   t = 0.5

4 The formula for the perimeter of a rectangle is

   P = 2(l + w)

   where P = perimeter of rectangle   l = length of rectangle
   and w = width of rectangle

   Find the perimeters of these rectangles.

   a l = 8 cm   w = 4 cm
   b l = 6.4 cm   w = 7.3 cm
   c l = 0.75 m   w = 0.56 m

5 The formula to convert a temperature from °C (degrees Celsius) to °F (degrees Farenheit) is

$$F = 1.8C + 32$$

where F = temperature (°F) and C = temperature (°C).

Use this formula to find F when

a $C = 20°$ **b** $C = 0°$ **c** $C = 28°$

6 The formula

$$T = S - 6.5K$$

can be used to work out the temperature as you go up a mountain where

T = temperature on the mountain (°C)
S = temperature at sea level (°C)
K = number of kilometres climbed vertically

Use the formula to find T when

a $S = 20$ $K = 2$

b $S = 26$ $K = 4$

c $S = 22$ $K = 2.6$

d Find the temperature 2 kilometres up the mountain when the temperature is 30 °C at sea level.

Consolidation Exercise 1

1 Find the missing numbers and rules in words for these sequences.

a 19   15   ___   7   ___

b 38   43   ___   ___   58

c 1   1   2   3   5   ___   ___

d 1   1   1   3   5   9   ___   ___

2 Adrian is making bridges with building bricks that click together.

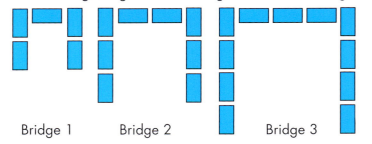

Bridge 1   Bridge 2   Bridge 3

a Copy and complete the table.

Bridge (*n*)	1	2	3	4
Number of bricks (*b*)				

b The number of bricks forms a sequence. What is the difference for this sequence?

c Write a rule connecting the bridge number and the number of bricks in words.

d Write a formula connecting the bridge number and the number of bricks.

3 The formula $P = 3a + 2h + d$

where P = total points scored
a = number of away games won
h = number of home games won
d = number of games drawn

is used to work out the points scored by hockey teams in the Big League.

Find P when $a = 4$, $h = 3$, $d = 2$

4 To work out how many sausage rolls (*s*) she needs to order for a party, Laurie multiplies the number of people (*p*) by 3 and adds 15.

She can use the formula below to work out how many sausage rolls to order:

$$s = 3p + 15$$

a Laurie invites 16 people to her birthday party. How many sausage rolls will she need to order?

b How many sausage rolls would be needed for 32 people?

5 To work out maximum heart rate when exercising, gym members use the formula

$H = 220 - a$
where H = heart rate a = age in years

a Kate is 56. What should her maximum heart rate be when exercising?

b Bill is 18. What should his maximum heart rate be when exercising?

Task 2: Sequences

Part A

- Open a new spreadsheet in Excel.
- In cell A1, key in 'Starting number'.
  In cell A2, key in 'Multiply by'.
  In cell A3, key in 'Add'.
- In cell A6, key in the formula = B1
  In cell B6, key in the formula = A6*B2+B3
  In cell C6, key in the formula = B6*B2+B3
  In cell D6, key in the formula = C6*B2+B3
- Look at the pattern in the formulas that you keyed into cells B6, C6 and D6.
  Key the next formula into cell E6.
- Enter the formulas for cells F6, G6 and H6.
- Try out your Sequence generator by putting the starting number 0 (put 0 in cell B1), multiply by 1 (put 1 in cell B2) and adding 1 (put 1 in cell B3).
  Describe the sequence that you have generated.
- Change the numbers in cells B1, B2 and B3 to generate the sequence
  1   2   3   4 ...
- Use your spreadsheet to complete the table. You may have to try different numbers before you get it right!

Sequence	Starting Number	Multiply by	Add
0 1 2 3 4 ...	0	1	1
1 2 3 4 5 ...	1		
2 4 6 8 10 ...			
1 3 5 7 9 ...			
5 10 15 20 25 ...			
2 4 8 16 32 ...			
3 8 13 18 23 ...			
8 18 28 38 48 ...			
3 3^2 3^3 3^4 3^5 ...			

Part B

- Use the sequence generator to create some sequences of your own. Before you enter these into the spreadsheet try to predict what the results are going to be. Was your prediction correct?

- Now write down the sequences for another pupil to try to find the rule that you used. Remember that you should keep the numbers reasonably small so that it is easier to try to find the values that generated the sequence.

Measures 1

In this chapter, I am learning to:
- carry out calculations involving areas and perimeters
- find the perimeters and areas of composite shapes
- use scale in maps and drawing.

Discussion 9.1

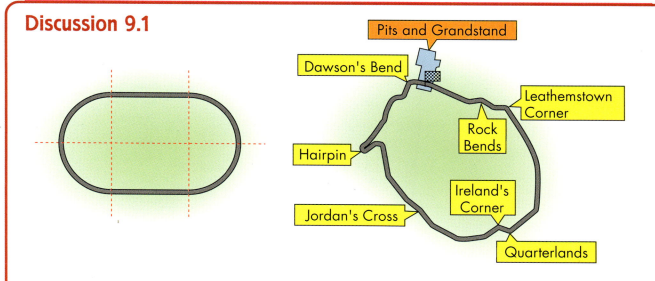

Look at the two diagrams above. What do they both show?

Are all race circuits the same shape? What type of events take place here? Can you name any other famous circuits in Ireland or Britain?

The total distance around a racecourse or circuit is known in mathematics as the **perimeter**. Most oval running tracks have a perimeter of 400 m.

Perimeter refers to the distance around the outside edge of any shape or area regardless of its shape. The perimeter of a square and rectangle can be found using formulae.

Perimeter of square = $4l$

Perimeter of rectangle = $2l + 2b = 2(l + b)$

where l is the length and b is the breadth.

Exercise 9a

1. Look at the perimeters of the circuits in the table.

Race circuit	Type of circuit	Distance
Silverstone	Grand Prix	5.141 km
	International	3.619 km
	National	2.638 km
	Stowe	1.281 km
Brands Hatch	Grand Prix	3.703 km
	Indy circuit	1.929 km

   a What is the difference in length between the longest and shortest circuits?

   b How many metres longer is the Grand Prix circuit than the International circuit?

   c A racer completes five laps of the Grand Prix circuit at Brands Hatch. What distance has he completed?

2. In a sports magazine a cricket square is said to measure 30 m by 23 m.

   a What is unusual about this statement?

   b An athlete is training by running around the cricket 'square' five times. How far does he run?

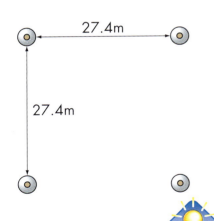

3. In a game of rounders the batsman runs around a circuit consisting of four bases placed in the shape of a square. If the distance between the bases is 27.4 m, how far will the batsman have to run to complete a circuit (ignore the length of the bases)?

4. Draw different circuits which could be used to play rounders using four bases. The length of the entire circuit must be 110 m.

5. A runner trains by running around a hockey pitch which is 91.4 m long and 55 m wide. He wants to run a distance of 1 kilometre. Suggest how he can use the hockey pitch to find a circuit which is as close to 1 kilometre as possible. Compare your answer with other pupils in the class.

Exercise 9b

1. Use the formulae given on page 82 to find the perimeter of shape **a** and **b**.

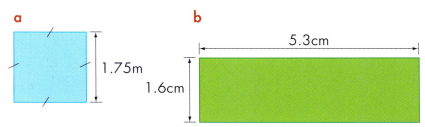

2. The perimeter of each shape is 48 cm. In each diagram calculate the missing length marked l.

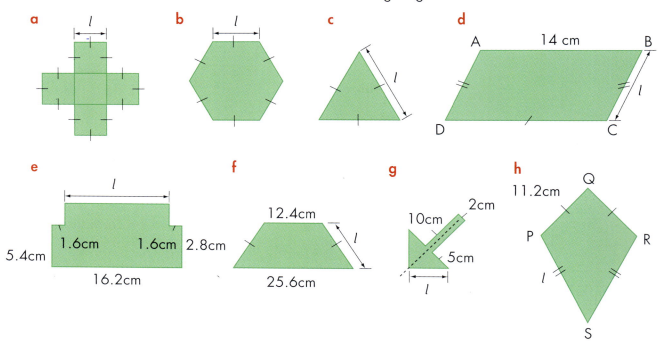

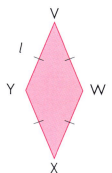

3. The perimeter of the rhombus VWXY is 17 m. Calculate the length of l.

4. The diagram shows the plan of a school playground. The headmaster wishes to put up a perimeter fence around the entire area, excluding the school gate.

   a. What length of fencing will be required?

   b. Round the answer in part **a** to two decimal places.

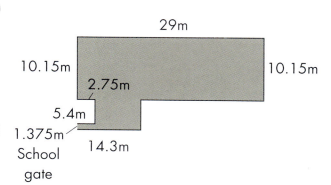

Discussion 9.2

Explain what is meant by the perimeter of a shape.

Explain what is meant by the area of a shape.

Devise a simple way to remember the difference between area and perimeter when you are asked to calculate them.

Area refers to the amount of **surface** inside a shape.

The area of some shapes are found using formulae.

Area of square = l^2 Area of rectangle = lb

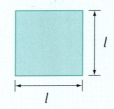 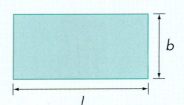

Area of triangle = $\frac{1}{2}bh$

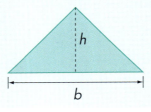

Activity 9.1

Exercise 9c

1 A music festival stage is made of square concrete slabs.

   a What is the area of the stage?

   b Sound cabling is placed around the perimeter of the stage. What total length of cable will be needed?

   c The concert organisers want to keep cost to a minimum by using the smallest amount of cabling. The area of the stage must remain constant.

      i   Draw different stage designs and find the one which would satisfy this requirement.

      ii Not all of the designs may be practical for holding the band's equipment. In your opinion, is the cheapest design the most practical?

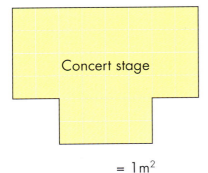

= $1\,m^2$

2 A garden centre has designs for five different patios. For each patio calculate

  a the perimeter of edging required to completely surround the area

  b the area, in square metres (round the answers to two decimal places where necessary).

i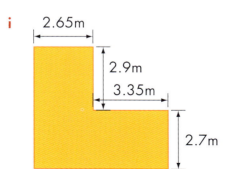

ii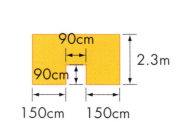

iii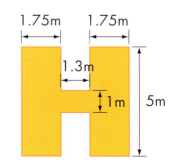

iv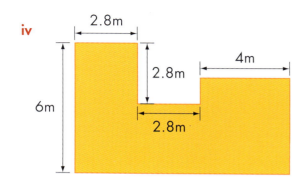

v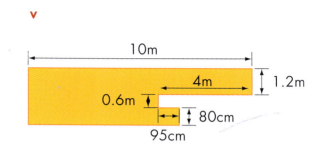

3 ABCD is a square of area 28 cm².

  a What is the length of each side? Give the answer to 2 d.p.

  b Use the answer from part a to find the perimeter of the square.

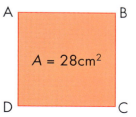

4 The perimeter of the triangular lawn is 55 m.

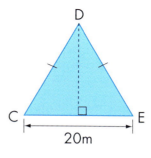

  a If CD = DE, calculate the length of each side.

  b Make an accurate scale drawing of the triangle using 1 cm to represent 1 m.

  c Measure the perpendicular height of the triangle accurately.

  d Use the answer in part c to calculate the area of the triangular lawn.

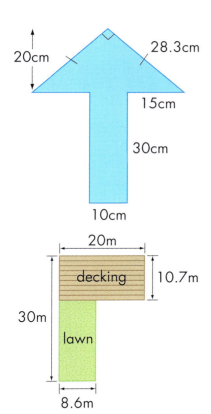

5 A road traffic sign is made from an isosceles right angled triangle and a rectangle.

  a What is the perimeter of the sign?

  b Find the area of the triangular top in square centimetres.

  c What is the total area of the metal needed to make ten similar signs?

  d The sign is cut from a large rectangular sheet with dimensions 42.5 cm by 55 cm. What area of each sheet is wasted?

  e What is the smallest rectangular sheet that the shape could be cut from to reduce wastage?

6 The diagram shows a plan of Damien's back garden.

  a Damien wants to put up a perimeter fence. What length of fencing (including gates) will he need?

  b Find the area of the lawn.

  c Find the area of the whole garden.

  d It takes 1 kg of lawn seed to sow 28 m². Lawn seed is sold in 2 kg boxes costing £11.99. How much will it cost to sow his lawn?

Activity 9.2

Discussion 9.3

An architects' ruler has eleven different scales 1 : 10, 1 : 20, 1 : 25, 1 : 33$\frac{1}{3}$, 1 : 50, 1 : 75, 1 : 100, 1 : 200, 1 : 250, 1 : 500 and 1 : 750

Why are so many different scales included on one ruler?

The scales on this ruler are written in ratio form. This method is very often used in atlases and maps.

What does 1 : 10 mean?

What is the actual length of a line measuring 12 cm on the page at this scale?

Another way of writing a scale is to use words, for example, 1 cm represents 8 km. What is the actual length of a line measuring 3 cm on the page using this scale?

The scale 1 cm represents 8 km can also be written as a ratio. How?

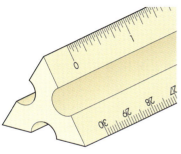

Example 9.1

A map has a scale of 1 : 75 000. The distance between two towns on the map is 2.4 cm. What is the actual distance between these places?

1 cm on the map represents 75 000 cm on the ground.

2.4 cm on the map will represent
75 000 × 2.4 cm = 180 000 cm = 1.8 km

Activity 9.3

Exercise 9d

1 Each of these lines is drawn to a given scale. Measure the line and write down the length it represents.

   a 1 cm to 10 cm _____

   b 1 cm represents 15 km _____

   c 1 : 20 _____

   d 1 : 100 ————————————————

   e 1 : 2500 ——————————————————

2 Using each of the given scales, draw lines representing the given lengths.

   a Scale 1 cm represents 15 m

      i 30 m   ii 22.5 m   iii 300 m   iv 97.5 m

   b Scale 1 cm to 3 km

      i 8.4 km   ii 15 km   iii 14.4 km   iv 47.4 km

3 A map is drawn to a scale 1:50 000.

   a What length is represented by a distance of 1 cm on the map?

      Copy and complete the following:

      1 cm represents _____ cm

      1 cm represents _____ m

      1 cm represents _____ km.

   b The distance between two towns is 15 km. How far apart will they be on the map?

   c Dave measures the distance from the forest to the town centre to be 6 cm on the map. What is the actual distance between them in kilometres?

4 The diagram shows a rough plan of a garden.

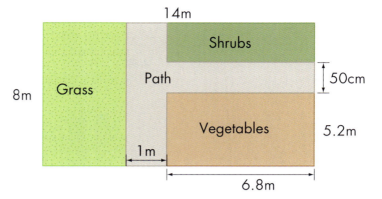

The garden plan has not been drawn to scale.

   a Use a scale of 1 : 200 to make a scale drawing of the garden.

   b Find the area of the shrub bed.

   c Calculate the actual area of the garden taken up by the path.

5 A rectangular room measures 2.7 m by 3.6 m.

   a Use a scale of 1:30 to calculate the scaled length and breadth of the room.

   b Carpet costs £87 per square metre. Calculate the cost of carpeting the room.

6 The rooms in these plans have been drawn to the given scale.

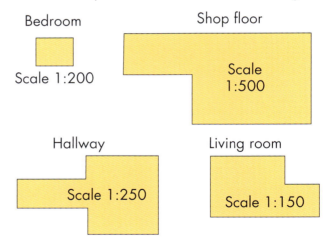

In each case

   a use the given scale to find the actual dimensions of the room

   b calculate the area of each of the floor plans.

Activity 9.4

Consolidation Exercise 1

1. What is the area of the base of a rectangular games console that measures 30.9 cm by 25.8 cm?

2. What is the area of each of the triangles?

   a   b

   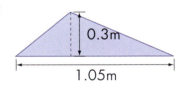

3. What is the area of a rectangle with dimensions 2.35 cm by 8.07 cm? Give your answer to

   a two decimal places

   b one decimal place.

4. A rectangular yard has an area of 25.2 m². The yard is 5.6 m long. Calculate its breadth.

5. On a map of Northern Ireland the scale used is 1 : 400 000.

   a The map distance, as the crow flies, between Ballymena and Omagh is 7.9 cm. What is the actual distance in kilometres?

   b The distance between Dungannon and Enniskillen is 27.2 km. What is the distance between the two towns on the map?

6. A rough sketch of a room plan has been drawn. Draw the plan accurately using a scale of 1 : 50.

   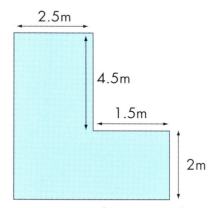

   Diagram not drawn to scale

7. On a building site plan a scale of 1 : 250 000 is used.

   a What width will a housing block be on the plan if it is 200 m in reality?

   b A road passing through the site is 1.5 km long. What length is this on the plan?

Task 3: Planning a Garden

This is a task about estimating so you will not be using a calculator. Where necessary, round any figures to make the calculations as easy as possible.

Mr and Mrs Johnston are planning a garden. They have made out the design and want to estimate the cost.

What size are the squares on the scale diagram?

Mr and Mrs Johnston have found out the prices for the different surfaces for their new garden.

Surface	Decking	Paving	Lawn (turf)	Path
Price	£67 per sq m	£28.50 per sq m	£2.45 per sq m	£3.75 per metre length

The trees and flowers that they want to plant will cost about £300.

Throughout this activity you must describe the method that you are using and show all calculations.

1 Copy and complete the table to work out the estimated cost of the garden.

Surface	Estimated area/length	Estimated cost	Total cost of each surface
Decking	m²	per sq m	
Paving	m²	per sq m	
Lawn	m²	per sq m	
Path	m	per metre length	

2 Work out an estimate for the overall cost by adding all the values in the last column of the table.

Add in the £300 that Mr and Mrs Johnston will pay for the flowers, trees and shrubs.

Show your working out.

3 Compare your answer for the estimated cost of the garden with others in the class.

Write down some reasons why your answers are different.

10 Fractions, Decimals and Percentages 1

In this chapter, I am learning to:

- understand relationship between fractions, decimals and percentages
  e.g. 25% = 0.25 = $\frac{1}{4}$, $\frac{37}{100}$ = 0.37 = 37%
- find a percentage of a quantity
- use a percentage key on a calculator.

Discussion 10.1

Billy says that $\frac{1}{4}$ of his teeth have fillings. What percentage is this?

Billy has 32 teeth. How many are filled? What fraction is not filled? What is this as a percentage? Billy's dentist advised him to reduce the number of sweets he eats. If Billy ate 30% less sweets after visiting the dentist, what is this reduction as a decimal? What is this as a fraction? Is $\frac{1}{3}$ the same as 30%? Explain your answer.

Example 10.1

Convert $\frac{2}{5}$ to a decimal and a percentage.

$\frac{2}{5} = \frac{20}{50} = \frac{40}{100}$

As a decimal this is 0.4

To convert decimals to percentages, simply multiply by 100%.

0.4 × 100% = 40%

Activity Sheet 10.1

Activity 10.1

Exercise 10a

SUS10a

1. Complete the table of fraction, decimal and percentage equivalences on SUS10a.

Shape	Fraction filled (in lowest terms)	Decimal fraction filled	Percentage filled

2 Complete this table on SUS10a.

Fraction	Decimal	Percentage
	0.5	
		10%
		1%
$\frac{3}{5}$		
	0.08	
$\frac{3}{100}$		
$\frac{47}{100}$		
	0.95	
		64%
$\frac{27}{30}$		

3 Find the odd one out.

a 25% $\frac{1}{4}$ 0.25   2.5

b $\frac{3}{4}$ 75%   3.4 $\frac{9}{12}$

c 0.1   1% $\frac{1}{10}$ $\frac{10}{100}$

Explain your answer for each.

4 Which of the following is the smallest?

a 40%   0.3 $\frac{2}{5}$

b 30% $\frac{1}{3}$ 0.35

Discussion 10.2

Fractions, decimals and percentages are all different ways of writing the same thing. One half ($\frac{1}{2}$) is the same as 0.5 (5 tenths) and 50% (50 out of 100).

What is $\frac{3}{10}$ the same as? What about 45%? What about 0.02?

Can a percentage ever be bigger than 100? If so, give an example of a suitable situation.

What is $1\frac{1}{2}$ as a decimal and as a percentage?

Sometimes it is more sensible to use one form rather than another.

Find examples of when it is best to use fractions.

When is it best to use decimals?

When is it best to use percentages?

Activity 10.2

Exercise 10b

1. The brain uses $\frac{1}{5}$ of the body's blood and oxygen. Write $\frac{1}{5}$ as
   a. a decimal
   b. a percentage.

2. Mobile phone ring tones make up 10% of the music industry's revenue. Write 10% as a fraction and as a decimal.

3. Ants make up 15% of the total mass of living creatures on Earth. What is this as a fraction in its lowest terms?

4. Two per cent of chickens in Britain are free range compared to 80% in France. What are these values as
   a. decimals
   b. fractions in their lowest terms?

5. Humans and cabbages have 57% of their genes in common. What is this as a decimal?

6. Mother tarantulas kill 99% of the babies they hatch. What decimal fraction survive?

7. When asked to write something with a new pen 19 out of every 20 people write their name. What is this as
   a. a percentage
   b. a decimal?

8. A typist's left hand does 56% of the typing. Write this as a decimal and as a fraction.

9. The Pacific Ocean covers $\frac{7}{25}$ of the Earth's surface.
   a. What is this as a percentage?
   b. What is it as a decimal?

10. A straw holds $1\frac{1}{2}$ teaspoons of water. What is this as
    a. a decimal
    b. a percentage of a teaspoon?

11. A rat can lift 116% of its body weight. What is this as a decimal?

12. Your mouth produces 1.8 pints of saliva each day.
    a. What is this as a mixed number of pints?
    b. What is it as a percentage of a pint?

Activity 10.3

Discussion 10.3

What does percent mean? What is 1% of £1? What about 2% of £1? How could you find 8% of £6?

What method would you use to find 10% of an amount of money? What is 10% of £80? What is 10% of £8.70?

Discuss with a partner how to find 20% of an amount. Try to find two different methods.

When 10% is known, 30%, 40%, etc. are easily found by multiplying by 3, 4, etc. Is this the best way to find 50%?

Compare 20% of £200 and 10% of £400. What do you notice? Explain your answer.

Mental Maths 10.1

Exercise 10c

1 Find
   a 10% of £4.50
   b 30% of £1.50
   c 20% of £0.70
   d 50% of £75

2 a How could 15% of an amount be found easily?
   b Find 15% of these amounts.
      i 80p   ii £2.40   iii £18   iv £72

3 a Describe how to find 75% of an amount.
   b Find 75% of these amounts.
      i £8   ii £20   iii 60p   iv £2.80

4 Find
   a 35% of £200
   b 45% of £9
   c 65% of £50

5 a Describe two methods to find 95% of an amount. Find 95% of £80 using both your methods.
   b Which method would you recommend?

6 Ant says 21% of £12 is £2.42 while Dick thinks it is £2.52. Who is correct? Explain your method.

7 a What percentage is equivalent to $\frac{1}{3}$?

b What percentage is equivalent to $\frac{2}{3}$?

c Find

   i $33\frac{1}{3}\%$ of £3
   ii $33\frac{1}{3}\%$ of £36
   iii $33\frac{1}{3}\%$ of £0.99
   iv $66\frac{2}{3}\%$ of £6
   v $66\frac{2}{3}\%$ of £9
   vi $66\frac{2}{3}\%$ of £33

8 Which is bigger: 30% of £4 or $33\frac{1}{3}\%$ of £3.60?

9 Pat's bank account is overdrawn by £200. If his bank charges him 12% interest on this amount how much more does he owe?

10 Eileen owes her credit card £180. As a minimum payment she must pay off 3% of this balance or £5, whichever is the greater. How much does she have to pay?

11 Kate buys a hairdryer advertised as £15 with 15% off. How much does she save?

12 Fill in the missing values.

   a 50% of _____ = £10
   b 25% of _____ = £3
   c 10% of _____ = 8p
   d 20% of _____ = £2
   e 1% of _____ = 25p
   f 40% of _____ = £4

Discussion 10.4

What is meant by tipping in restaurants? Generally, 10% is added as a tip in Ireland and the UK. Why do you think 10% was chosen? In other European countries many restaurants already add the tip to your bill and holidaymakers end up tipping twice. In some countries e.g. Japan, on the other hand, tipping is often seen as an insult.

Activity Sheet 10.4

Activity 10.4

Discussion 10.5

What is 15% of 200? In maths what operation does 'of' suggest?

Use a calculator to find 15% of 200. Write down carefully what you input. Did you use the calculator's % key? Try again and record what you input.

Exercise 10d

Use your calculator's % key to answer these questions. Write down exactly what you key into your calculator. The first one is done for you.

1. Find 15% of £300   Answer: £45; 300 × 15%
2. Find 27% of £40
3. Find 7% of £30
4. Find 65% of 90 m
5. Find 12% of 1200 km
6. Find 77% of 350 litres
7. Find 2.5% of 40 pages
8. Find 125% of 60 hours

Discussion 10.6

How can a percentage be converted to a decimal? What is 45% as a decimal? What about 5%? What about 17.5%? When asked to find a percentage of an amount most people don't bother with their calculator's percentage key. How could you find 65% of £48?

Example 10.2

Find 42% of 3000 km.

Change 42% into a decimal by dividing by 100

42% = 0.42

Remember 'of' means multiply. So 42% of 3000 km is found by keying

0.42 × 3000 = into your calculator. The answer is 1260 km.

Exercise 10e

1. Change these percentages into decimals.
   - **a** 27%
   - **b** 31%
   - **c** $7\frac{1}{2}$%
   - **d** 150%
   - **e** 11%
   - **f** 1.1%

2. **a** Find 14% of £75
   b Find 75% of 60

3. 69 000 spectators watched Manchester United play Everton. If 72% of the crowd were Manchester United supporters, how many is this?

4. There are 12 000 schoolchildren in Youngtown. 73% travel by bus to school, 8% by taxi, 1.5% by train, 4% cycle, 9% are given a lift by parents and the rest walk.
   - **a** What percentage walk to school?
   - **b** How many pupils **i** take the bus **ii** travel by taxi **iii** take a train **iv** cycle **v** are given a lift **vi** walk?

5. Academy College has 550 pupils. 20% are in Year 8, 28% are in Year 9, 18% are in Year 10, 22% are in Year 11 and the remainder are in Year 12.
   - **a** What percentage of pupils is in Year 12?
   - **b** How many pupils are in each year group?
   - **c** Fifty-four per cent of the pupils are boys. How many girls are there?

6. There are four million CCTV cameras in the UK. It is estimated that 95% of them are privately owned. How many is this?

7. The population of Northern Ireland is 1.75 million. Children (under 16) make up 22% of the population, adults (16–64) make up 64% and the elderly (65+) make up the rest.
   - **a** What percentage of the population is classed as elderly?
   - **b** In Northern Ireland, how many
     - **i** children
     - **ii** adults
     - **iii** elderly people are there?
   - **c** The population is expected to rise by 4% over the next five years. How many more people is this? Why do you think the population is predicted to rise?

8. In 2006 the people in Northern Ireland threw out 1.6 million tonnes of rubbish from their homes. Disposable nappies made up 4% of this waste. How many tonnes is this? What could be done to reduce this waste?

9. **a** Find 117% of 200
   b Without any working out, write down the answer to 200% of 117.

Activity 10.5

Activity 10.6

Mental Maths 10.2

Consolidation Exercise 1

Write all fractions in their lowest terms.

1.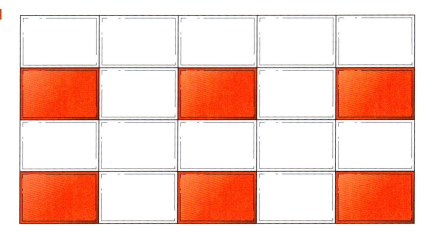

   a What fraction of tiles are red?
   b What is this as a percentage?
   c What is this as a decimal?

2. Write $2\frac{1}{4}$ metres as a decimal number of metres.

3. Nigel pays 40% tax.
   a What is this as a decimal?
   b What is it as a fraction in its lowest terms?

4. Serge paid a 30% deposit on a new car.
   a What fraction is this?
   b What is this as a decimal?

5 A bicycle is advertised as $\frac{1}{3}$ off in a sale.

   a What percentage is this?

   b What percentage is paid?

6 a Seventeen percent of humans are left handed. What fraction is this?

   b What decimal fraction of people are not left handed?

   c What decimal fraction of people are right handed?

7 Chilinda scored 35 out of 50 in a test.

   a Reduce this fraction to its lowest terms.

   b What percentage did Chilinda achieve?

   c What is this as a decimal?

8 One quarter of a number is 12. What is 50% of this number?

9 Sixty per cent of a number is 24. What is the number?

10 Jamie sits a French test. It is marked out of 80. To get a C grade you need to get at least 60% of the marks. How many marks does Jamie need to get a C?

11 One quarter is equivalent to 25%. One eighth is half of a quarter.

   a Write $\frac{1}{8}$ as a percentage and as a decimal.

   b What is $\frac{7}{8}$ as a percentage?

12 Take 10% off £25. Now add 10% of this amount back on. What do you notice? Can you give an explanation?

Measures 2

In this chapter, I am learning to:
- calculate the volume of cubes, cuboids and triangular prisms
- calculate the surface area of prisms
- calculate composite volumes.

Discussion 11.1

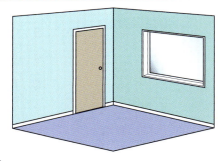

What is meant by volume?

Why is volume measured in cubic units?

Since the cube is the basic measure of volume, which shapes is it easiest to find the volume of?

Exercise 11a

Find the volume of the following shapes. Each cube is 1 cm³.

1
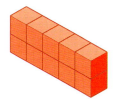

2
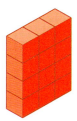

3
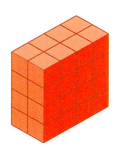

4
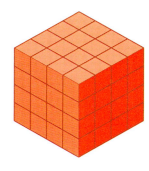

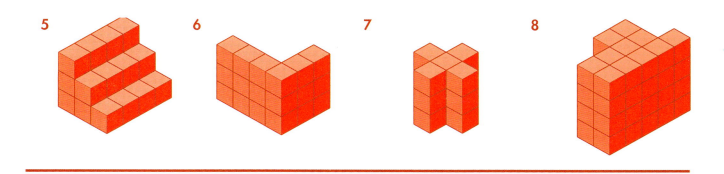

The volume of a cuboid can be found using a formula, when you know the length, breadth and height.

Volume of cuboid = $l \times b \times h$

Volume of a cube = l^3

Example 11.1

Find the volume of the storage box.

Volume of cuboid = $l \times b \times h$
= $10.5 \times 10 \times 3.1$
= 325.5 cm^3

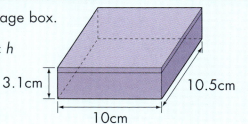

Exercise 11b

Calculate the volume of each of these cubes and cuboids.

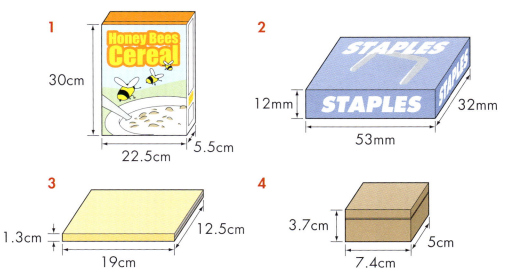

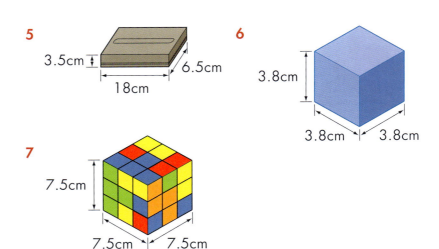

5 3.5cm, 18cm, 6.5cm

6 3.8cm, 3.8cm, 3.8cm

7 7.5cm, 7.5cm, 7.5cm

Discussion 11.2

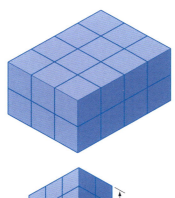

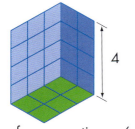

area of cross section = 6 cm²
volume = 6 × 4 = 24 cm²

Kris and Kirsty are trying to find the volume of this 3-D shape. Kris says that one way to find the volume is by counting the cubes. What is the volume of the prism using this method?

Kirsty says she knows a much better method to find the volume for any prism.

Kirsty finds the area of the cross section of the prism.

Area of cross section = 6 cm²

To find the volume of the prism she multiplies the area of the cross section by the height, $h = 4$ cm.

She finds the volume of the shape to be 24 cm³.

In Example 11.1, the volume of a cuboid was found using $v = l \times b \times h$. Is this the same as the method Kirsty is using? Explain your answer.

Kirsty says that the method she uses is better. Why might she think this?

Volume of prism = area of cross-section × height
The volume of a cylinder can also be found using this method.

Example 11.2

Volume of cylinder = $A \times h$
= 22.5×9
= $202.5 \, cm^3$

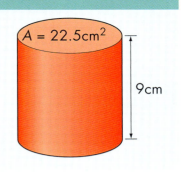

Exercise 11c

Calculate the volume of these solids.

1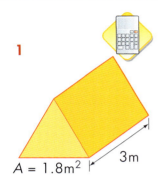

2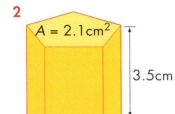

3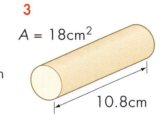

4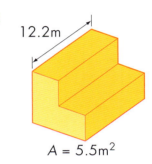

5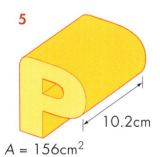

6

7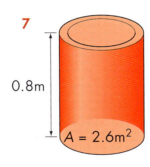

8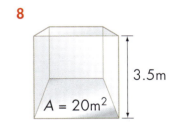

9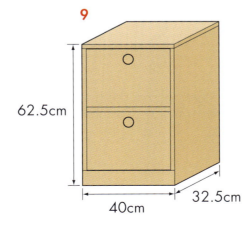

10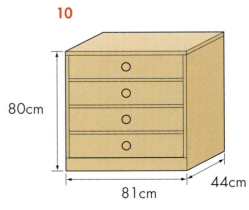

Activity 11.1

Activity 11.2

Exercise 11d

1   A medallists' stand is constructed for sports day.

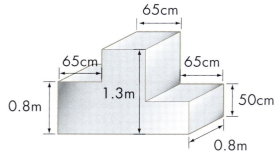

Calculate the total volume taken up by the stand in m².

2   Fern has just bought a combination wardrobe for her bedroom. Calculate the total storage space available.

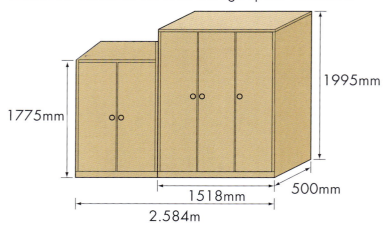

3   Rick is making a ramp for his back door. Calculate the volume of cement he will need in cubic metres.

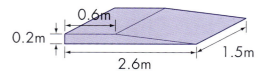

4   A company have designed a new logo for their firm. The logo is shown below. Calculate the volume.

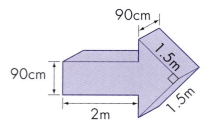

Discussion 11.3

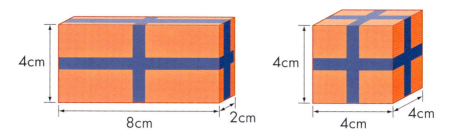

What is meant by the surface area of a shape?

The pictures show gifts which have the same volume. Does it take the same amount of wrapping paper to cover them? Give reasons for your answer.

How would you find the surface area of the cube shown?

Find the surface area of the cuboid.

Exercise 11e

Find the total surface area for each of these containers. Diagrams are NOT drawn to scale.

1

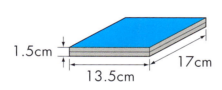

2

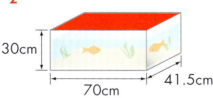

3

4

5 The diagram shows the plastic display packaging around a selection of coffee sachets. The package is open at both ends. The diagram has NOT been drawn to scale.

   a Sketch a net of the sleeve.

   b What is the total area of plastic needed to make this package?

107

6 Thom is designing an *open topped* toy box in CDT. The net of his box is shown.

Calculate the surface area of the box.

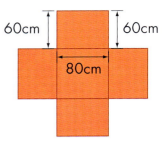

7 Grace is covering a shoe box with coloured wrapping paper for a shoe box appeal.

The base of the open shoe box measures 34.2 cm long by 20.4 cm wide by 14 cm high.

The lid of the box measures 34.2 cm long by 20.4 cm wide by 4 cm high.

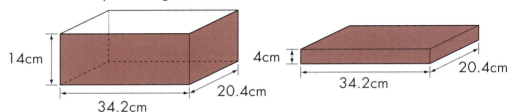

  a Calculate the exact amount of paper required to cover the entire base of the box.

  b What area of paper is needed to cover the box lid?

  c Find the total amount of paper needed altogether.

  d If a sheet of wrapping paper measures 70 cm by 0.5 m, how many sheets will Grace need to buy?

8 The cereal cartons both hold the same mass of cereal but are a different shape.

  a Ignoring the cardboard needed for flaps, calculate the surface area of each box.

  b Which box has a bigger surface area, and by how much is it bigger?

9 John draws the net of a cube and calculates the total surface area. His answer is 600 cm².

  a What is the area of each square face?

  b What is the length of each side of the cube?

10 Draw a net of a cube which has a surface area of 96 cm².

Discussion 11.4

The Government would like us to be more environmentally friendly. Suggest some ways manufacturers can help to reduce waste packaging.

Activity 11.3

Consolidation Exercise 1

1

Internal Dimensions	Width	Depth	Height
	124.968 cm	82.296 cm	103.632 cm
Overall Dimensions	Width	Depth	Height
	143.256 cm	94.488 cm	121.92 cm

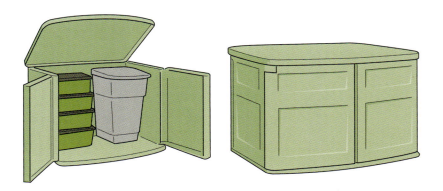

The diagram shows a storage shed. Use the dimensions given to answer parts **a** and **b**.

a Calculate the internal volume of the storage in cubic metres.

b Calculate the overall volume taken up by the shed in cubic metres.

c Explain what the difference between these two volumes represents.

2 Find the volume of these containers.

a $A = 43 \text{ cm}^2$ b $A = 24.375 \text{ cm}^2$

10.8cm

13.8cm

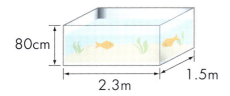

3 A fish tank is shown.

   a Draw a net of the tank marking on the length, breadth and height in centimetres.

   b Calculate the total surface area of the tank.

4 The diagram shows the side view of a ramp.

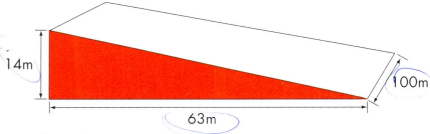

Find its volume.

5 a Draw a net of an open top box which has a volume of 36 cm³.

   b For the net you have drawn, calculate the surface area.

   c Repeat for other possible dimensions of a box having the same volume.

   d What are the dimensions of the box which uses the least card?

6 A rectangular box has a volume of 792 000 cubic centimetres. If the length of the box is 1.6 m and its breadth is 90 cm, what is its height?

7 a A cube contains 343 ml of juice. What is the length of each side of the cube?

   b What is the area of a face of the cube?

Task 4: Waste Reduction

A packaging company has been asked to produce a net for a storage box with a volume of 24 000 cubic centimetres. The dimensions of the box can be chosen by the company. Each net produced has to be cut from a square sheet of length 1 metre. The company does not have to add flaps as the boxes will be heat sealed. The only condition is that the waste material cut from each sheet must be kept to a minimum.

Your task is to work as a production team to investigate a possible net which would be suitable.

1. Think about, and provide suggestions to your team for, different possible dimensions of boxes having a volume of 24 000 cm^3. Discuss the suggestions made by each member of your team. Are all the suggestions sensible and practical for the design of the storage box? Decide which box dimensions you are going to investigate. Give each team member a different box size to investigate.

2. Draw different possible nets for the box. Remember the net will have to fit onto a sheet which is 1 m^2. Any nets which do not meet this condition will have to be binned!

3. Calculate the area taken up on the sheet by the net of your box. What area of the sheet is wasted?

4. Compare the amount of waste with the other designs from your team members. Which net wastes the smallest amount of card?

5. Report back to the other teams in the class. Is your box the best for wastage reduction?

12 Time

In this chapter, I am learning to:

- interpret information from different types of timetables
- perform calculations involving days, hours, minutes and seconds
- realise the effect time zones have on travellers and businesses throughout the world.

Discussion 12.1

Tempus fugit, a common Latin expression meaning 'time flies' is frequently used as an inscription on clocks. Have you ever considered how much our lifestyles and routines are dictated by time?

Make a list of different ways in which time plays an important factor in your life. Compare your list with others in the class. Are they similar?

Calendars and timetables play an important part in our daily schedules. Timetables usually display times using the 24 hour clock.

Exercise 12a

This calendar only shows the first three months of the year. Use this calendar to answer Questions **1** to **4**.

1 Write down the days of the week for each of these dates.

  a 13th January

  b 14th February

  c 16th March

  d 1st April

2 Does this particular year have 365 or 366 days? Explain how you found your answer.

3 On what day will 1st May fall in this particular year?

4 How many Sundays will there be in April?

5 Here is an extract from a flight timetable, showing flight times from Belfast International to Edinburgh.

Belfast Intl–Edinburgh – summer (25th March to 27th October)
All times are local

Travel Day	Belfast Intl to Edinburgh Dep.	Arr.	Edinburgh to Belfast Intl Dep.	Arr.
Mo-Fr	07.35	08.25	06.25	07.15
Mo-Sa	15.00	15.50		
Mo-Fr	18.05	18.55	13.50	14.40
Mo-Fr	21.10	22.00	16.50	17.40
Mo-Fr			19.55	20:45

a i In summer how many flights are available, Monday to Friday, from Belfast to Edinburgh?

ii How many flights are available Monday to Friday from Edinburgh to Belfast?

b Frank is in Edinburgh and he was booked on the 13.50 flight to Belfast. Frank does not arrive at the airport until 13.45 and it is too late to check in. How long does he have to wait until the next flight departs to Belfast?

c Valerie takes the 07.35 flight from Belfast and returns on the same day on the 19.55 flight from Edinburgh. She parks her car in the short stay park at Belfast International Airport. Assuming the return flight lands on schedule, how long will her car be parked for if she arrives 2 hours before the flight departure time and takes 20 minutes to return to her car on the way home?

d Calculate the total number of days the summer timetable is in operation. Both of the given dates are inclusive.

Discussion 12.2

When travelling abroad, reading timetables can be more complicated. Here is a flight time from London to Venice.

London dep. 11.15   Venice arr. 12.45

It appears that this flight takes 1 hour 30 minutes when the actual flight time is $2\frac{1}{2}$ hours. Can you explain why this is?

The times given in the timetable are always based on **local time** and this can cause confusion. Time is measured in relation to British time (**Greenwich Mean Time** or **GMT).**

The map of the world shows the standard time zones.

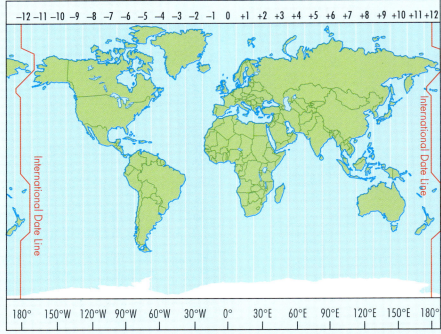

A time zone is a region of the Earth that uses the same standard time, usually referred to as the local time. Most adjacent time zones are exactly one hour apart, and calculate their local time from Greenwich Mean Time (GMT).

Exercise 12b

The diagram shows the time difference, in hours, in various cities compared to GMT.

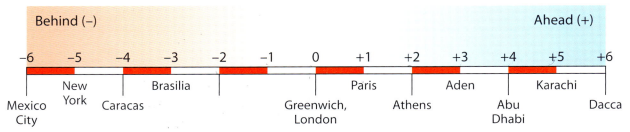

1. What is the time difference between Mexico City and Abu Dhabi?

2. It is 19.00 hours in Paris. What time is it in New York?

3. How many hours is Karachi time ahead of Brasilia?

4. A plane takes off from Paris at 16.30 hours, local time. It lands in New York at 18.00 hours, local time, on the same day. How long did the flight take?

5 The table on SUS12b shows the time in some cities of the world when it is 5:24 pm Tuesday in London GMT. Calculate the time difference between these countries and Greenwich. Use + to indicate the number of hours ahead of GMT and − to indicate the number of hours behind GMT.

CITY/Country	Time	Time difference
Baghdad, Iraq	8:24pm TUE	
Bangkok, Thailand	11:24pm TUE	
Nanjing, China	2:24am WED	
Istanbul, Turkey	7:24pm TUE	
Karachi, Pakistan	9:24pm TUE	
Jakarta, Indonesia	11:24pm TUE	
Athens, Greece	7:24pm TUE	
Hanoi, Vietnam	11:24pm TUE	
Hyderabad, India	9:24pm TUE	
Recife, Brazil	1:24pm TUE	
Hong Kong, China	12:24am WED	
Melbourne, Australia	2:24am WED	

6 The Live Earth 24-hour worldwide event staged eight concerts on seven continents in a bid to highlight global warming. The concert started in Aussie Stadium, Australia at 1 am GMT.

a What was the local time in Australia?

b The timetable of events for each continent is shown. Use the internet, or otherwise, to find the start times of the concerts in local time for each of the different continents.

4 am (GMT)	Toyko
11 am (GMT)	Johannesburg, South Africa
11.30 am (GMT)	Shanghai
1 pm (GMT)	Hamburg
1.30 pm (GMT)	London
7.30 pm (GMT)	New York
8 pm (GMT)	Rio de Janeiro

Activity Sheet 12.1

Activity 12.1

In Northern Ireland we switch to British Summer Time (BST), which is an hour ahead of GMT. Greenwich Mean Time does not switch to summer time. This is referred to as Daylight Saving Time.

Activity Sheet 12.2

Activity 12.2

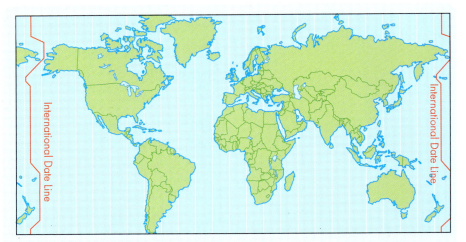

The International Date Line causes time confusion amongst airline travellers as well. Australia is approximately 17 hours ahead of the United States and you have to cross the International Date Line when traveling from one country to the other. This means that if you leave the United States on a Saturday, you will arrive in Australia on a Monday. On your return from Sydney to Los Angeles, if you leave Sydney on a Saturday afternoon, you will arrive approximately 12–13 hours later but it will be the same Saturday, in the morning. You actually 'go back' in time because you cross the International Date Line going in the opposite direction. If the line is crossed from east to west, a day is added. If the line is crossed from west to east, a day is subtracted.

Exercise 12c

1 The table below shows flights from Derry to London Stansted.

Flight	Departure	Arrival
111	07.00	08.25
112	16.05	17.25
113	20.05	21.25
114	21.10	22.30

a What is the departure time of the first afternoon flight?

b What is the flight time for each journey?

c Georgina arrives at the airport at 6.35 pm. How long will she have to wait for the next flight going to London?

2   The itinerary for a cruise ship is show in the table. Passengers join the cruise at Athens and leave it at Venice.

Port	Arrive	Duration of stay	Depart
Athens	Sat 14th July 1600		
Istanbul	Sun 15th July 2000	24 h	a
Rhodes	Wed 18th July 0600	b h	Wed 18th July 1830
Limassol	Thurs 19th July c	$5\frac{1}{2}$ h	Thurs 19th July 1930
Haifa	Fri 20th July 0700	$36\frac{1}{2}$ h	d
Venice	Mon 23rd July 0900		

In the itinerary there are four missing pieces of information.

a   What is the departure day, date and time for the ship to leave Istanbul?

b   For how long is the ship anchored in Rhodes?

c   At what time does the ship arrive in the port of Limassol?

d   What time is the departure from Haifa?

e   For how many nights are passengers on board the cruise liner?

f   How long does the sea journey from Athens to Istanbul take?

g   At what time of day does the ship always sail from one port to another? Can you suggest a reason for this?

Activity 12.3

Activity Sheet 12.3

Discussion 12.3

In school why is it important to be punctual for lessons? Why is good timekeeping an important factor for employers? What different methods do employers use to keep a time check on their employees and ensure good timekeeping?

Exercise 12d

1. Employees in a factory have to clock in and out during working hours. The working day is as follows.

   Start time 08.45; Breaktime 10.00–10.15; Lunch 13.00–13.30; Finish time 17.15

   a Calculate the total number of hours worked during a normal day.

   b John's clock card is as follows.

   Start 08.56; Breaktime 09.57–10.24; Lunch 12.50–13.39; Finish time 17.03.

   Use this information to calculate how many minutes John has wasted when he should have been working.

   c Assuming John wasted this number of minutes each day, how much of his employer's time would he have wasted at the end of a five-day week?

   d If John continues to waste this amount of time each week, how much time will he have wasted by the end of a year? (Assume that he works 48 weeks each year.) Why would this be important to an employer?

2. The table shows the legal maximum weekly working hours for men and women in different countries.

Country	Legal maximum hours
Austria	45.5
Belgium	48.0
Czech Republic	46.5
France	35.0
Ireland	48.0
Italy	48.0
Latvia	48.0
The Netherlands	48.0
Poland	46.5
Spain	48.0
Sweden	48.0
United Kingdom	Up to 60

   a Which countries have a maximum of a 48-hour week?

   b Breen is a security guard in Ireland. He works five 12-hour shifts per week. Is this legal according to the published table? Give a reason for your answer.

c Hugh works in a frozen food factory in the United Kingdom. Each week he works four 12-hour shifts. Is this legal according to the published table? Give a reason for your answer.

d In the UK, there can be longer working hours. What are the disadvantages of working this length of time each week?

e What effect will the length of the working week in France have on the country and workforce? Use the internet to help you find ideas.

3 Jan works a $37\frac{1}{2}$-hour week from Monday to Friday.

a She works the same number of hours each day. How many hours is this?

b Jan has a one hour lunch break which is not included in the $37\frac{1}{2}$ hours. She begins work each day at 08.45. Calculate the time she will finish work.

4 Robert has a job in a factory where he normally works a 40-hour week. Sometimes he works overtime.

a What is meant by the term 'overtime'?

b Robert works from 08.00 to 16.00 from Monday to Friday and works from 08.00 to 12.00 on Saturday. How many hours has Robert worked altogether?

c How many hours overtime has he worked?

d Robert earns £7.30 per hour. His overtime pay per hour is $1\frac{1}{2}$ times this amount. How much does he get paid for each hour of overtime?

e How much will Robert get paid in total for the week's work?

5 A job is advertised as shown.

a What does flexible mean?

b Fran is interested in applying for this job but she would like to work a three-day week. If she works the same number of hours each day, how long would she have to work every day?

c Assuming she is given the job, what time will she finish work if she starts at 08.30 and has a half hour break for lunch?

Situation vacant

Person required to work 18.75 hours per week, flexible hours

Call 0207 555 1234

Activity Sheet 12.4

Activity 12.4

Consolidation Exercise 1

Chapter 12: Time

1 The timetable shows the buses which operate between Coleraine and Magherafelt during the week. Use the timetable to answer the questions.

Notes					Sch							UN	F
Coleraine, Buscentre	0650			0730		0825	0940	1040	1100	1305	1340	1515	
Ballylagan, Church	0707						0957	1057			1357		
Killaig, Crossroads										1320			
Garvagh, Diamond				0803		0845			1119	1335		1535	
Swatragh, Main Street			0805			0855							
Kilrea, Church Street	0728		0805	0815			1018	1118		1420			
Upperlands, Station Road	0747				0835			1037		1440			
Maghera, Cinema	0755	0759	0815	0828		0843	0906		1045		1448		
Maghera, Station Road							0903		1135			1552	
Magherafelt, Buscentre	0824		0854				0920		1155		1518	1608	

Sch – School Terms only
F – Fridays Only
UN – Operates University Terms only

Notes:		Sch						UN	F
Coleraine, Buscentre	1540	1540	1550	1705	1710		1740	1745	
Ballylagan, Church			1607					1802	
Killaig, Crossroads	1555			1725					
Garvagh, Diamond	1610	1610		1740		1810			
Swatragh, Main Street	1621								
Kilrea, Church Street			1628	1750		1830			
Upperlands, Station Road			1647	1807	1810				
Maghera, Cinema			1655	1818					
Maghera, Station Road					1825				
Magherafelt, Buscentre			1720	1844	1840				

Saturday	
Notes:	C
Coleraine, Buscentre	1705
Ballylagan, Church	1722
Kilrea, Church Street	1745

C – Via Aghadowey Station and Cullycapple
Sch – School Terms only

a At what time does the 06.50 bus from Coleraine Bus Centre arrive at Maghera Cinema?

b What time does the first bus leave Coleraine to go direct to Magherafelt?

c How long does this journey take?

d How long does the 07.30 bus from Coleraine take to reach Garvagh?

e Compare the length of time taken to get from Coleraine to Garvagh on the 15.40 school bus to your answer for **d**.

f Rory lives in Coleraine and he wants to meet up with his school friends in Maghera to go to the cinema.

  i What is the latest bus he can catch from Coleraine?

  ii The film begins at 19.15. How long will Rory have to wait in Maghera?

2 Doreen lives in Upperlands and she wants to visit her friend in Magherafelt hospital.

a How many buses travel from Upperlands to Magherafelt during the course of a day?

b If visiting time is from 14.00 to 16.00, which bus will Doreen have to take from Upperlands? How long does this journey take?

c It takes 10 minutes to walk from the Bus Centre to the hospital. How long will Doreen actually have to visit her friend in hospital?

3 Harry has a part time job in a chip shop. He starts work on Friday at 5.00 pm finishing at 2.00 am on Saturday. On Saturday he also works from 16.00 hours to midnight.

a How many hours does Harry work for?

b How much will he earn if he is paid £5.75 per hour?

13 Mass

In this chapter, I am learning to:
- measure and record masses using the most appropriate unit
- use metric and imperial measures of mass
- convert from one metric unit of mass to another and know how this relates to place value
- carry out calculations relating to mass and value for money.

Discussion 13.1

Look at the objects in the picture. Which object do you think is the heaviest?

Which is the lightest? If you were to place them in order from the heaviest to the lightest, how would you arrange them?

The smallest unit of mass commonly used is the milligram and the largest measure is the tonne.

1 kilogram (kg) is the equivalent of 1000 grams (g). A litre of water has a mass of 1 kg.

1 gram is equal to 1000 milligrams (mg).

1 tonne is equal to 1000 kg.

Why are the metric conversions from one unit of mass to another easy to remember?

Activity 13.1

121

Example 13.1

To convert kilograms to grams we multiply by 1000 as there are 1000 g in 1 kg.

Convert 2.36 kg to grams.

2.36 kg = 2.36 × 1000 g
        = 2360 g

To convert grams to kilograms we use the reverse operation and divide by 1000 as there are 1000 g in 1 kg.

Convert 5470 g to kilograms

5470 g = 5470 ÷ 1000 kg
       = 5.47 kg

Mental Maths 13

Mental Maths 13

Exercise 13a

1 Arrange these weights in order of size starting with the lightest.

   a 6.7 kg, 6000 g, 6.08 kg, 6100 g
   b 9560 mg, 9.6 g, 0.9 kg, 9275 mg

2 The masses of articulated lorries are recorded in tonnes. Change these masses to tonnes.

   a 35 000 kg
   b 23 700 kg

3 The mass of an average egg is 58 g. What is the total mass of 12 identical eggs?

4 The weight of an aluminium drink can was 16.55 g in 1992 and in 2005 a similar can weighed 14.7 g.

   a How many grams lighter is the 2005 version?
   b Change the answer in part **a** to milligrams.

5 In Italy the mass of school bags was recorded. The heaviest bag had a mass of 16.3 kg and the average mass of a school bag was 11.5 kg.

   a Calculate the difference between the heaviest mass and the average mass.
   b Harry's school bag weighs 750 g less than the mass of the heaviest bag. What is the mass of Harry's bag?
   c Claire's school bag is 945 g more than the average mass. Find the mass of her bag.

6 A litre of milk has a mass of 1.027 kg. A litre of water has a mass of 1 kg.

   a How many grams heavier is a litre of milk compared to a litre of water?

   b A creamery can for holding milk holds 45 litres. Calculate the mass of milk needed to fill the can.

Discussion 13.2

Why do shoppers purchase organic food rather than other foods?

Is organic food more expensive than non-organic varieties?

Example 13.2

Compare the price of these apples.

0.94 kg of organic apples cost £1.64

0.45 kg of non-organic apples cost £0.54

To compare both prices find the price for 1 g of each type of apple.

Organic

0.94 kg = 940 g   940 g cost 164p

1 g costs 164 ÷ 940p = 0.17p (rounded to two decimal places)

Non-organic

0.45 kg = 450 g   450 g cost 54p

1 g costs 54 ÷ 450p = 0.12p

The organic apple is 0.05p per gram more expensive than the non-organic variety. This would be 5p more for 100g of apples.

Exercise 13b

1. 500 g of organic plums cost £1.99 and 750 g of non-organic plums cost £2.96.

   a Find the cost of 250 g of the organic and non-organic plums, to the nearest penny.

   b What is the difference in cost of 250 g of each type?

2. The home economics teacher asks her class to decide which of the following packs of cherry tomatoes is better value.

   a How much will 500 g of the organic cherry tomatoes cost?

   b Which type of cherry tomato is more expensive? How much more expensive is it for 500 g of the more expensive ones?

3. A 750 g container of non-organic mushrooms costs £1.18. Organically grown mushrooms are sold at 64p for 200 g.

   a Calculate the cost of buying 1 kg of organically grown mushrooms.

   b Calculate the cost of buying 1 kg of non-organic mushrooms, to the nearest penny.

   c How much more expensive is the organically produced product?

4. Jane buys a bag of apples each week. If she buys a bag of organic apples she has to pay £2.49 for a bag of six apples. If she buys a bag of ordinary apples she gets an equivalent mass for £1.19. Calculate how much more expensive it would be for her to buy organic apples over the period of a year.

5. A kilogram of organically grown pears costs £2.58. A kilogram of non-organic pears costs £1.18. If the average weight of a pear is 150 g, use this information to find

   a the cost of an organic pear

   b the cost of an ordinary pear.

   c What is the price difference in pence?

6 a Look at the prices of the two bags of non-organic baking potatoes.

Is it cheaper to buy the larger bag? Show calculations to support you answer.

b Use the information in the picture to calculate the cost of 1 kg of organic baking potatoes.

c Compare the price of a kilogram bag of non-organic baking potatoes with a kilogram of organically produced potatoes. Which one is cheaper and by how much per kilo?

7 A head of pre-packed non-organic broccoli costs 54p for 0.458 kg. A head of organic broccoli costs £1.28 for 0.428 kg.

a Find the cost of 1 kilogram of each type of broccoli.

b How much more expensive is it to buy a kilogram of organic broccoli?

Activity 13.2

Activity 13.3

Discussion 13.3

Very often we still use the older imperial measures.

Can you name any of the imperial measures of mass which are still widely used? Who might still use imperial units?

Find out where these measures originated from.

Which unit of measure do you think it is better to use, metric or imperial? Give reasons for your answer.

To convert between imperial and metric units these equivalences are used.

2.2 lb = 1 kg

1 lb = 16 ounces

so 16 × 2.2 lb = 35.2 ounces = 1 kg

1 kg = 1000 g = 35.2 ounces and so
1 ounce = 1000 ÷ 35.2 = 28.4 g

This is taken as 28 g **to the nearest gram**.

1 ounce is approximately equal to 28 g.

If 1 ounce is approximately equal to 28 g then it is easy to find how many grams are equivalent to 1 **pound** (lb).

1 lb = 16 ounces = 454.4 g. This is taken as 454 g to the nearest gram.

1 lb is approximately equal to 454 g

Example 13.3

A bag of sweets has a mass of 4 ounces (oz). How many grams is this approximately equivalent to?

Taking 1 oz = 28 g   4 oz = 28 g × 4 = **112 g**

Example 13.4

A baby weighs 5 lb 6 oz. What is the weight in kilograms?

Two separate conversions need to be carried out.

a 5 lb to g   1 lb = 454 g   so 5 lb = 454 g × 5 = 2270 g

b 6 oz to g   1 oz = 28 g   so 6 oz = 28 g × 6 = 168 g

The total mass in grams = 2270 + 168 = 2438 g = 2438 ÷ 1000 kg = 2.438 kg

Exercise 13c

1 A large packet of washing powder has a mass of 4.75 kg. The pack contains 50 scoops of washing powder.

  a How much does one scoop of washing powder weigh in grams?

  b Convert the mass of one scoop of powder into ounces. Give your answer correct to the nearest ounce.

2 A parcel has a mass of 0.908 kg.

  a How many grams is this?

  b Taking 1 lb = 454 g, work out the mass of the parcel in pounds.

3 A cake recipe requires 140 g of sugar, 450 g of flour and 250 g of margarine. The scales Mrs Baker has only weigh in pounds and ounces. Approximately how many ounces of each ingredient should she weigh out?

4 A bag of potatoes weighs 5 lb. What is the approximate mass in kilograms?

5 A new born baby weighs 5 lb 10 oz. Convert this weight to kilograms and grams.

6 Sean had a mass of 3.27 kg at birth and his twin brother Seamus had a mass of 3 kg.

  a How many grams was Sean heavier than his brother?

  b Convert the answer to **a** into ounces.

7 The mass of a toy tanker is 5.6 kg. Work out how many pounds this is equal to.

8 In America the mass of children's schoolbags has a maximum value.

Look at the table and change the masses into metric units.

School grade	Max mass of schoolbag
Kindergarden to Grade 4	3 lb
Grades 5 to 8	4 lb
Grades 9 to 12	5 lb

The Government is encouraging people to have a 'healthy weight' to cut down the risks of cancer, strokes, heart disease and diabetes. One way of deciding if a person is at risk is by calculating his body mass index (BMI). BMI is a measure of body fat based on height and weight for adults.

BMI	Category
≤18.5	underweight
18.5 to 24.9	normal
25 to 29.9	overweight
>30	obese

BMI is calculated using the formula

$$BMI = \frac{weight}{height^2}.$$

The weight must be in kilograms and the height in metres.

Example 13.5

Find the BMI of an adult of height 160cm and 65 kg. In which category is this?

BMI = $\frac{65}{1.6^2}$ = $\frac{65}{2.56}$ = 25.39

This BMI indicates that the person is overweight.

Exercise 13d

Use this method to calculate the BMI for the following people and decide which category they fit into.

1. Fergal is 153 cm tall and weighs 70 kg.
2. Shona is 153 cm tall and weighs 55 kg.
3. Ian is 1.6 m tall and weighs 50 kg.
4. Lucy is 1.5 m tall and weighs 40 kg.
5. Robbie is 1 m 60 cm tall and weighs 80 kg

Increasing emphasis is being placed on eating a healthy diet. Foods which are high in salt, fat and sugar levels can lead to serious health problems such as heart attacks, high blood pressure and diabetes.

The Guideline Daily Amounts (GDA) help consumers understand the **nutritional** information on food labels. The GDAs inform consumers about the amount of **fats**, **saturated fats**, **sugars**, **calories**, **carbohydrates**, protein, fibre, **salt** and sodium that are considered healthy for an everyday diet.

The table shows the recommended GDA for teenagers.

	Girls 11–14 years	Boys 11–14 years
Energy (calories)	1850	2200
Fat (g)	70	85
Saturated fat (g)	25	25
Carbohydrate (g)	230	275
Total sugars (g)	90	110
Protein (g)	41	42
*Sodium (g)	2.4	2.4
*Salt (g)	6	6

*You will usually see sodium included in the nutrition information on food labels. Many products also say how much salt they contain. salt = sodium × 2.5.

> **Discussion 13.4**
>
> Nutritionists refer to 'hidden fats, salt and sugar'. What do you think this means? How can reading the food label help you become health conscious?

Activity 13.4

Exercise 13e

1 The table shows nutritional information on a packet of sea salt crisps and a packet of roast chicken crisps.

	Sea salt Per 35g:	Roast chicken Per 35g:
	712kj	712kj
	171kcal	166kcal
Protein	2.0 g	2.2 g
Carbohydrate	18.7 g	18.5 g
of which sugars	0.1 g	0.6 g
Fat	10.5 g	9.9 g
of which saturates	1.3 g	1.2 g
Fibre	1.6 g	1.5 g
Sodium	0.2 g	0.4 g
Salt	0.5 g	0.9 g

During a school day Jim eats a packet of sea salt crisps for his break and two packets of roast chicken crisps at lunch time.

a Calculate the total amount of fat, in grams, that Jim has eaten.

b What is the total amount of saturated fat that he has eaten?

c How much salt is contained in the three bags of crisps?

d How many milligrams of sugar are in the packet of roast chicken crisps?

2 The table shows the maximum amounts of salt children should have in a day:

Age	Maximum amount of salt
1 to 3 years	2 g a day
4 to 6 years	3 g salt a day
7 to 10 years	5 g a day
11 and over	6 g a day

A teaspoonful of salt is approximately 6 g.

a What fraction of a teaspoon of salt are 4 to 6 year olds allowed in a day?

b For how many days should a teaspoon of salt last 1 to 3 year olds?

c Copy and complete the table in milligrams.

3 Three cracker biscuits contain 8.3 g of carbohydrate.

a How many milligrams of carbohydrate are contained in one cracker? Give the answer to the nearest milligram.

b A box of 36 crackers has a total mass of 125 g. If the empty box has a mass of 2600 mg, find the mass of one cracker.

4 One hundred grams of porridge contains 8.5 g of fat.

a How many grams of fat will be in a single serving of 27 g?

b A serving contains 30% of the 3 g of oat fibre suggested per day to help lower cholesterol. How many milligrams is this?

Activity 13.5

Consolidation Exercise 1

1. A packet of 24 ginger nut biscuits has a mass of 200 g.
   a. What is the mass of one biscuit in grams?
   b. Change the mass of a biscuit to milligrams.
   c. The biscuits are packed in boxes of 50 to distribute to supermarkets.
      What is the total mass of the biscuits in kilograms?
   d. The manufacturer has decided to change the mass of the packet from 200 g to 250 g. How many biscuits will be in the new sized packet?

2. A bakery is making an order of sausage rolls for a party. On average each sausage roll contains 28.5 g of sausage meat and 25 g of flour.
   a. How many sausage rolls can be made from 1 kg of flour?
   b. How much flour will be needed to make 150 sausage rolls?
   c. The bakery orders 4.5 kg of sausage meat to make 150 sausage rolls. How much sausage meat will be left over?
   d. How many *more* sausage rolls could be made from the left over meat?

3. A cake recipe requires 140 g of sugar. How many such cakes can be made from a 1 kg bag of sugar?

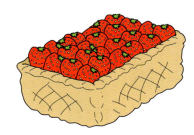

4. Small punnets are filled from a basket. Each punnet contains 250 g of strawberries. How many punnets can be filled if the mass of strawberries in the basket is
   a. 3 kg b. 4.75 kg c. 5.2 kg
   d. How many more grams of strawberries would be needed to fill another complete punnet in part **c**?

5. Jake's gran has just bought a metric set of scales. She is making bread and her recipe says she needs 6 ounces of flour. Change this to grams for her.

6. Peter weighs 113 kg. Convert his weight to stones and lb. (14 lb = 1 stone)

7. Frank weighs 12 st 13 lb and is 5 ft 9 inches tall.
   a. Convert his weight to kilograms.
   b. Convert his height to metres. (1 foot = 12 inches; 1 inch = 2.54 cm)
   c. Calculate his BMI.
   d. Would you say Frank is a healthy person? Give a reason for your answer.

14 Fractions, Decimals and Percentages 2

In this chapter, I am learning to:

- multiply a whole number by a fraction
- calculate fractions of a whole number quantity resulting in a decimal answer rounded to two decimal places
- solve problems using equivalence between fractions, decimals and percentages
- calculate with percentage in relevant contexts.

Discussion 14.1

Pete says the sum of $\frac{2}{8}$ and $\frac{3}{8}$ is $\frac{5}{8}$. Nina says the sum should be $\frac{5}{16}$. Who is correct?

How could you find the difference between $\frac{1}{4}$ and $\frac{2}{3}$?

Exercise 14a

1. Find the sum of these fractions.
   a $\frac{2}{7}$ and $\frac{3}{7}$
   b $\frac{5}{12}$, $\frac{3}{12}$ and $\frac{1}{12}$
   c $\frac{1}{10}$, $\frac{7}{10}$ and $\frac{5}{10}$

2. Find the difference between these pairs of fractions.
   a $\frac{3}{4}$ and $\frac{1}{4}$
   b $\frac{7}{8}$ and $\frac{2}{8}$
   c $\frac{7}{6}$ and $\frac{6}{6}$

3. Jack and Vera are sharing a pizza. If Jack eats $\frac{5}{8}$ of the pizza and Vera eats the rest, how much pizza does Vera eat?

4. Violet and Sean are sharing a packet of sweets. If Violet eats $\frac{2}{9}$ of the sweets and Sean eats $\frac{4}{9}$ what fraction have they eaten themselves?

5. Find
   a $\frac{1}{4} + \frac{3}{8}$
   b $\frac{1}{2} + \frac{1}{5}$
   c $\frac{3}{7} + \frac{5}{14}$
   d $\frac{2}{3} + \frac{1}{6}$

6. Find
   a $\frac{3}{4} - \frac{1}{2}$
   b $\frac{7}{12} - \frac{1}{3}$
   c $\frac{4}{10} - \frac{1}{4}$
   d $\frac{7}{8} - \frac{2}{5}$

Discussion 14.2

What operation does the word 'of' suggest in mathematics?

$\frac{1}{4} \times 12$ is the same as $\frac{1}{4}$ of 12. What is $\frac{3}{4}$ of 12?

What is $\frac{5}{8} \times 32$?

Example 14.1

What method could we use to find $\frac{3}{7} \times 21$?

$$\frac{3}{\cancel{7}_1} \times \cancel{21}^3 = 9$$

Exercise 14b

1. Find

   a $\frac{2}{7} \times 56$ 　　b $\frac{7}{8} \times 24$ 　　c $\frac{4}{9} \times 81$

   d $\frac{5}{6} \times 84$ 　　e $\frac{7}{8} \times 192$ 　　f $\frac{5}{12} \times 480$

   g $\frac{3}{4} \times 108$ 　　h $\frac{4}{9} \times 216$ 　　i $\frac{6}{11} \times 2651$

   j $\frac{5}{9} \times 4545$

2. Only $\frac{1}{9}$ of an iceberg's volume is above water. What volume of a 97 200 m³ iceberg is beneath the water?

3. The area of Alan's garden is 135 m². The lawn takes up $\frac{4}{9}$ of the garden. What is the area of the lawn?

4. The fuel tank in Fernando's car is $\frac{5}{18}$ full. The tank capacity is 72 litres. How much fuel has he left?

5. It is estimated that $\frac{17}{250}$ of Northern Ireland's population of 1 700 000 is under 5. How many people is this?

6. Alison spent $\frac{5}{12}$ of her £108 savings on a coat and $\frac{3}{16}$ on a blouse. How much of her savings did she spend on each item?

7. Mary and Joe had 72 sums to do. Mary got $\frac{3}{8}$ of her sums wrong while Joe got $\frac{5}{9}$ of his right. Who got more sums right and by how many?

8. Olwen earns £3750 each month.

   a If she loses $\frac{1}{3}$ to deductions (tax, national insurance and pension) how much remains?

   b Of Olwen's remaining pay, $\frac{8}{25}$ is spent on mortgage repayments. How much now remains?

   c Olwen saves $\frac{5}{8}$ of what remains. How much is this?

   d Olwen spends $\frac{2}{3}$ of whatever is left. How much is this?

Discussion 14.3

In a $\frac{1}{3}$ off sale how much would an item priced at £99 sell for?

What about an item priced £100? What is different in this case?

Problems involving money should always be rounded to two decimal places (i.e. to the nearest penny) unless you are told otherwise. In general it is sensible and practical to round most answers to two decimal places.

Example 14.2

Find $\frac{2}{7}$ of £16 correct to two decimal places.

Multiply 16 by 2 to get 32, then divide by 7. Since an answer to two decimal places is required it is necessary to work to three decimal places and round to two decimal places. Divide 32.000 by 7 as follows.

$$7 \overline{)3\,^32\,.\,^40\,^50\,^10} = 4.57 \text{ to 2 d.p.}$$
$$0\,4\,.\,5\,7\,1$$

£4.57

Exercise 14c

Round answers to two decimal places where necessary.

1 In a $\frac{1}{3}$ off sale what price is paid for goods advertised at the following prices?

   a a bike costing £170

   b a wok costing £25

   c a drum kit costing £499

2 Liz earns £699 per week. If she is given a pay rise of $\frac{1}{4}$, what are her new weekly earnings?

3 Tom's new mobile phone is $\frac{2}{3}$ the thickness of his old one. If his old phone was 23 mm thick, what is the thickness of his new phone?

4 Internet credit card fraud in the UK rose by $\frac{4}{11}$ in the first six months of 2007. If the previous figure was £194 million, what is the latest figure?

5 The rate of VAT is equivalent to $\frac{7}{40}$.

   How much VAT is payable on these items?

   a a Blu-ray disc player costing £299

   b an HDTV costing £675

   c an MP3 player costing £89

   d a digital camera costing £161

6 Lloyd received £85 for his birthday. He spends $\frac{9}{16}$ of his money, gives $\frac{2}{7}$ to his sister and saves the rest.

   a What fraction does he save?

   b How much money does he save?

Fractions of quantities other than money need to be calculated also. When the division is not exact rounding is often needed. Answers are usually rounded to two decimal places as in Exercise 14c.

Discussion 14.4

How could you find $\frac{3}{4} \times 7$?

What is $\frac{5}{8}$ of 10?

What is $\frac{3}{4} \times 93$?

If Walter lives three miles from school and has travelled $\frac{3}{5}$ of the way, how far has he gone?

Exercise 14d

In this exercise round all answers to two decimal places. Find

1 $\frac{1}{4}$ of 17 m

2 $\frac{2}{5}$ of 17 cm

3 $\frac{2}{3}$ of 20 kg

4 $\frac{3}{7}$ of 36 km

5 $\frac{1}{9}$ of 31 cm

6 In Year 8 Tessa threw the shot 7 m. By Year 10 she could throw it $\frac{2}{9}$ further.

   a How far could she throw the shot in Year 10?

   b What is $\frac{11}{9}$ of 7 m?

7 Sebastian is training to run a marathon. He ran a total of 43 miles last week. This week he ran $\frac{3}{13}$ further. How far did he run this week?

8 Abigail bought a 3.7 m length of material to make curtains. If she wasted $\frac{2}{9}$ of the material, how much did she use?

9 Lewis' fuel tank has a capacity of 70 litres. If it is $\frac{5}{12}$ full, how much fuel remains?

Example 14.3

Many decimals are easily changed into mixed numbers or fractions.

Write 1.5 as **a** a mixed number **b** an improper fraction.

a $1\frac{5}{10}$ or $1\frac{1}{2}$ **b** $\frac{15}{10}$

Discussion 14.5

Why would it be useful to write decimals in the way shown in Example 14.3?

Describe an efficient method of finding 5.2 times 500.

What about 1.25 × 12?

Give an example of your own to show how rewriting a decimal in this way would be useful.

Exercise 14e

1 Rewrite these decimals as mixed numbers.
   a 1.3   b 2.9   c 3.25   d 1.75   e 3.7 cm

2 Rewrite these decimals as improper fractions.
   a 1.5   b 2.3   c 1.25   d 1.03   e 2.15   f 1.85 m

3 Rewrite these mixed numbers as decimals.
   a $1\frac{1}{4}$ b $2\frac{1}{2}$ c $3\frac{3}{10}$ d $4\frac{92}{100}$ e $5\frac{1}{5}$

4 Rewrite these improper fractions as decimals.
   a $\frac{5}{2}$ b $\frac{9}{4}$ c $\frac{18}{10}$ d $\frac{140}{100}$ e $\frac{25}{4}$

5 Find 2.5 times
   a 16   b 20   c 42   d 120   e 3

6 Find 3.25 times
   a 4 kg   b 20 cm   c 16 litres   d £12   e 260 g

7 Twelve point five percent of 120 pupils have brown eyes. Fifteen pupils have green eyes. The rest have blue eyes. What decimal fraction have blue eyes?

8 Jenny put £300 into a savings account. After one year she had $\frac{11}{10}$ of her initial investment. How much money was now in her account?

Discussion 14.6

Many companies offer employees overtime. What does this mean? Why and when might overtime become available? Why would employees be prepared to work extra hours and shifts? If Kelli earns £10 an hour and is paid overtime at time and a half, how much does he earn for overtime worked? Johnny earns £8 an hour. If overtime is paid at time and a quarter, what is this rate as an improper fraction? Find the hourly rate of pay for Johnny's overtime.

Activity 14.1

Discussion 14.7

Susie has ten colouring pencils in her pencil case. Three are red, two are yellow and five are green. What fraction of the pencils is each colour? What are these fractions as decimals? What are these decimals as percentages?

Sami scored 28 marks out of 42 in a French test. What is this as a fraction in its lowest terms? What is this as a decimal and as a percentage?

What rule can be used to convert any fraction to a decimal?

What is $\frac{5}{8}$ as a decimal?

What is $\frac{7}{20}$ as a percentage?

What is $\frac{7}{15}$ as a percentage?

Activity 14.2

Exercise 14f

1. Convert these fractions to decimals, then convert the decimals to percentages (answer to two decimal places where appropriate).

   a $\frac{2}{5}$ b $\frac{12}{40}$ c $\frac{3}{7}$ d $\frac{9}{11}$ e $\frac{5}{3}$

2. Convert these decimals to fractions.

   a 0.03   b 1.08   c 0.92   d 1.6   e 0.64

3. Convert these percentages to fractions.

   a 33%   b 75%   c 61%   d 112%   e 0.8%

Activity 14.3

Example 14.4

A calculator can be used to simplify fractions.

Typing

gives , which means $\frac{2}{3}$.

What would a calculator showing

 represent? $3\frac{4}{5}$

Exercise 14g

1. Use your calculator to simplify these fractions.

   a $\frac{3}{9}$ b $\frac{5}{125}$ c $\frac{32}{80}$ d $\frac{16}{12}$ e $\frac{12}{5}$ f $\frac{114}{95}$

2. Convert each of your answers in Question 1 to decimals and give answers to two decimal places where appropriate.

3. Convert the fractions in Question 1 to percentages and give answers to two decimal places where appropriate.

Discussion 14.8

The results of a 2003 survey into young people in Northern Ireland found that over $\frac{2}{5}$ (41%) of all pupils live in households where adults smoke inside the house. Why do you think 41% has been written as $\frac{2}{5}$? Do you think this proportion has increased or decreased in the last few years? Comment.

Example 14.5

Put these in ascending order.

0.52 $\frac{32}{60}$ 55%

Choose a common format and write down equivalences that can be compared easily. Decimals or percentages are most sensible. Changing to decimals gives

0.52, 0.53 (to two decimal places) and 0.55.

The answer is then
0.52, $\frac{32}{60}$, 55%.

Remember always to give the original values, not the converted ones.

Exercise 14h

1. Write down a fraction, a decimal and a percentage between $\frac{1}{2}$ and 0.75

2. Arrange these in ascending order.

   a $\frac{2}{7}$, 27%, 0.3

   b $\frac{5}{3}$, 1.7, 165%

   c 0.73, $\frac{7}{9}$, 38% of 1.93

   d $\frac{3}{4}$ of 24, 60% of 28, 0.22 × 82

3. Alex scored the following test marks. English $\frac{18}{25}$, Maths 79%, Science $\frac{39}{50}$, French $\frac{12}{15}$ and History $\frac{24}{33}$.
   Arrange these marks in descending order.

4. Stephen says Liverpool have a 21% chance of winning the league, Jamie says they have a $\frac{2}{11}$ chance and Peter says their chance is 0.2. Put these chances in ascending order.

5. 15 600 people voted in an election. Ed received 23% of the vote, Al received $\frac{3}{13}$ of the vote, Bo received $\frac{5}{12}$ of the remaining votes and Fi received the rest. How many votes did each person receive?

Discussion 14.9

A supermarket uses bread as a 'loss leader'. What is a 'loss leader'? The supermarket reduces the cost of a loaf of bread from 80p by 30%. What price is the loaf reduced to?

Prudence put £200 into a savings account. If her savings increased by 6% after one year how much did she have? Her savings increased by 5% the following year. Why is this rate less than the previous one? How much are her savings now worth? Why is it important to save?

Exercise 14i

Give answers to two decimal places where appropriate.

1. Increase
   a £32 by 8%
   b 25 kg by 3%
   c 62 m by $33\frac{1}{3}$%
   d 40 minutes by 12.5%
   e £1.6 million by 22%

2. Decrease
   a 500 kg by 19%   b £35.99 by 13%   c 87 mm by 43%
   d 18 500 spectators by 6%   e £2.3 million by 14.5%

3. Both packs of cereal cost the same. Which is the best value?

4. In 2004 a total of 129 522 criminal offences were recorded in Northern Ireland.

   If this figure fell by 8.8% the following year, how many offences were recorded?

5. In 2003, 73 396 commercial and cargo flights flew out of the two main airports in Belfast. By 2005 this figure had increased by 15.8%.

   a What was the increased figure?
   b Why did you not get a whole number of flights?
   c In 2005, 56.1% of these flights left from the International Airport. How many flights was this?
   d How many flights left from George Best Belfast City Airport in 2005?

6. Tessa threw her javelin 13% further than Sandra. If Sandra threw 61.08 m, how far did Tessa throw?

7. Arthur joined a slimming club and lost 15% of his weight in three months. If he weighed 97 kg when he joined, how much did he weigh at the end of three months?

8 Mahmood deposited £3500 in a savings account in 2006 for two years. If he earned 5.5% interest in the first year and 6.7% interest in the second year, how much was in his account after two years?

9 Catriona borrowed £3500 from her bank to pay for a new bathroom. She agreed to repay the loan over 12 months incurring a 7.9% interest charge. How much did this £3500 loan cost her?

Consolidation Exercise 1

1 If you go blind in one eye you only lose about $\frac{1}{5}$ of your vision. What percentage of your vision remains?

2 Five percent of our teeth is water.
   a What is this as a decimal?
   b What is this as a fraction?

3 85% of a particular make of car is recyclable. What is this as a fraction?

4 Find $\frac{2}{5}$ of 90.

5 Find $\frac{1}{4}$ of 32 m correct to the nearest centimetre.

6 Sally has a pack of eight balloons. Two of the balloons are red.
   a What is this as a fraction in its lowest terms?
   b What percentage are red?
   c What decimal fraction are not red?

7 Which of these is 0.3 the same as? 3%, 30% or $33\frac{1}{3}\%$

8 In a sale a bicycle costing £320 has 7.5% off. If Bob buys one of the bicycles
   a what percentage of £320 does he pay?
   b What is this percentage as a decimal?
   c Multiply £320 by your decimal answer to find how much Bob paid.

9 A 3.25 m length of wood is shortened by 12%. How long is the shortened length of wood?

Task 5: Standby

The average household in the UK uses 3880 units of electricity but this could be reduced by making a few simple changes to our lifestyle.

Write a few sentences explaining why we might want to use less electricity.

In this task we will consider the effect of switching off appliances rather than using 'standby'.

The first column in the table shows the power used by some household appliances while on standby for 1 hour. This is measured in watts.

Appliance	Power (watts)	Per day	Per year	Units per year
CD player	9.7			
DVD player	4.2			
Clock	1.7			
Burglar alarm	13.7			
Microwave	2.9			
Computer	1.7			
Printer	5.0			
Cable/Satellite box	11.7			
Internet terminal	10.6			
Games box	1.3			
TV	7.6			
Cordless phone	3.0			
Answering machine	2.6			

- Complete the second column showing how much power each appliance uses in a day.
- Complete the third column showing how much power each appliance uses in a year.
- To complete the fourth column divide each value in the third column by 1000 to give the number of units of electricity each appliance uses in 1 year while on standby. Round your answer to one decimal place if necessary.
- Draw a suitable chart to display this information. You could use an Excel spreadsheet to do this.

- The average household in the UK wastes approximately 9% of all the electricity used by having appliances on standby.

If electricity costs 8p per unit, how much money does the average household in the UK waste per year?

- Customers can pay their electricity bills in a number of different ways. One way is to use 'direct debit'. This means that a fixed amount is paid out of the customer's bank account each month. If it is too much, that amount will be given back at the end of a certain amount of time. If it is too little, more will be paid to make up the difference.

Customers can save around 3% of their total bill if they pay by direct debit.

Use the information given in the last section to work out how much money the average household in the UK can save by paying by direct debit.

Find out about other ways of paying electricity bills in Northern Ireland. Go to http://www.nieenergy.co.uk/.

Write a short report about what you found out in this task.

15 Negative Numbers

In this chapter, I am learning to:
- use a number line to show negative numbers
- understand and use negative numbers in context
- add and subtract negative numbers.

Discussion 15.1

Amy is counting backwards from 10

10   9   8   7   6   5   4   3   2   1   0

She stops at zero as she thinks there are no numbers less than zero.

Is this correct?

Can you continue her counting?

When does it stop?

Numbers less than 0 are called **negative numbers.**

The first whole negative number is −1. This is read as 'minus 1'.

Numbers greater than 0 are called **positive numbers.**

Positive numbers sometimes have a + sign.

45   + 7.3   and   +476 are all positive numbers.

Zero is neither positive or negative.

Numbers can be shown on a number line.

Example 15.1

Use the number line to find these.

a 7 more than –3

Start at –3 on the number line. Move 7 steps in the + direction.

You end at 4 so 7 more than –3 = 4 (or +4)

b 5 less than 2

Start at 2 on the number line. Move 5 steps in the – direction.

You end at –3 so 5 less 2 than = –3

Activity 15.1

Activity Sheet 15.1

Exercise 15a

1 Write these numbers in ascending order (smallest first).

   a 8   7   –2   6   –6

   b –7   –13   7   0   –5

   c –8   –4   –12   –1   1

   d –20   –10   –5   –40   –21

   e –3   –9   –7   –11   –5

2 Use a number line to help you with this question. Write down the number that is:

   a 3 more than 7   **b** 3 less than 2

   c 4 more than –3   **d** 5 less than 1

   e 6 less than 0   **f** 5 more than –9

   g 8 less than 7   **h** 4 more than –4

   i 7 more than –2

3 Your number line is too small to use for these!

Write down the number that is:

   a 4 less than –10   **b** 20 less than 10

   c 50 more than –90   **d** 15 more than –5

   e 6 more than –24   **f** 18 less than 8

   g 2 less than –101   **h** 7 more than –28

   i 200 less than –400

145

4 Write in the missing numbers in these sequences.

a 2   1   0   ___   ___
b –9   ___ –7   ___   –5
c 30   20   ___ ___   ___
d ___ ___ 0   5   10
e ___ ___ 0   100   ___

Discussion 15.2

We use negative numbers when measuring temperature.

What temperature would we have on a really cold day in Northern Ireland?

What about a very cold day in Iceland?

Example 15.2

The temperature in Belfast is 3 °C. In Warsaw the temperature is –5 °C. What is the difference between the temperatures?

Find 3 °C and –5 °C on the thermometer.

Count the number of steps that it takes to get from 3 to –5.

There are eight steps so the difference between the temperatures is 8 °C.

Exercise 15b

You can use the thermometer or number line to help you with this exercise.

1 The temperature at 6 pm in Belfast was 6 °C. By midnight the temperature had fallen by 7 °C. What was the new temperature?

2 The temperature at 6 am in Aberdeen was –5 °C. By 11 am the temperature had risen by 4 °C. What was the new temperature?

3 The average temperature for January in Anchorage, Alaska is –7 °C.

   The average temperature for January in Belfast is 5 °C.

   What is the difference in the average January temperature for these two places?

4 The temperature at midnight in Moscow was –23 °C. By 10 am it has risen to –9 °C. By how many degrees did the temperature rise?

5   The table shows the temperatures in different places at midnight on a day in February.

Place	Coleraine, Northern Ireland	Glencoe, Scotland	Omsk, Russia	Winnipeg, Canada	Alicante, Spain
Temperature (°C)	4	−8	−15	−18	7

   a   Put these temperatures in order starting with the coldest.
   b   How much warmer was it in Alicante than in Coleraine?
   c   How much colder was it in Glencoe than in Coleraine?
   d   How much colder was it in Coleraine than in Alicante?
   e   What was the difference in temperature between Omsk and Winnipeg?
   f   What was the difference in temperature between Winnipeg and Coleraine?
   g   At 6 am the temperature in Omsk has increased by 9 °C. What is the new temperature?
   h   At 6 am the temperature in Winnipeg has increased by 6 °C. What is the new temperature?

6   The coldest temperature ever recorded on earth was −89 °C (at Antarctica on 21 July 1983).

   The hottest temperature ever recorded on earth was 58 °C (at Azizia, Lybia on 13 September 1922).

   Calculate the difference between these two temperatures.

Activity 15.2

Activity Sheet 15.2

Discussion 15.3

Negative numbers are used in other situations. Can you suggest any examples?

If you have £10 in your bank account and you withdraw £50 from the autobank then you will have −£40 in the bank. This means that you owe the bank £40.

When you put money into your account you have made a **deposit**.

When you take money out, this is a **withdrawal**.

The amount of money in your account at any time is your **balance**.

If you owe the bank money, your account is **overdrawn**. Why do banks allow customers to become overdrawn?

If you have −£40 in your account and you put £100 in, what is your new balance?

Sometimes buildings have floors below ground and they are given negative numbers.

Floor –2 would be two floors below the ground floor.

Divers might also use negative numbers to represent the depth of the sea.

–100 m would be 100 metres below sea level.

Exercise 15c

1. Ricky has £18 in his bank account. He uses his debit card to buy a T-shirt costing £23. What is his balance now?

2. Robyn has a balance of –£42. She deposits £150 into her account. What is her new balance?

3. A department store has a notice to show what is on each floor of the building.

Floor	Department
3	Furniture, Kitchenware, Curtains, Fabrics
2	Menswear, Childrens' clothes, Baby clothes
1	Womens' clothes, Designer labels, Accessories, Handbags
G	Perfume, Cosmetics, Footwear
–1	Electrical goods, Sports equipment, Toys
–2	Car park

a. Julia takes the lift from the car park and goes up four floors. Which floor does she arrive at?

b. Mark has just bought some baby clothes and wants to go to the car park. How many floors does he need to go down?

c. Zoe goes from the car park to the top floor. How many floors does she go up?

d. Shelley is looking at handbags and then takes the lift to look at tennis racquets. How many floors does she go down?

4 The table shows the heights above sea level of different places in the world.

Place	Antrim Plateau, Northern Ireland	The Dead Sea	Mount Blanc, France	Schiphol Airport, Amsterdam	Japan Trench, Pacific Ocean
Height above sea level (metres)	360	–418	4808	–4	–9000

What is the difference in height between

a The Antrim Plateau and Mont Blanc

b The Dead Sea and Mont Blanc

c The Dead Sea and Schiphol Airport

d The Japan Trench and the Antrim Plateau?

5 Victoria, David and Greg are playing a game using this playing board.

They throw a six-sided die to tell them where to move their counters. The die has 1, 2, 3, –1, –2, and –3 on the sides.

a Victoria is on the –2 square and throws a 3 on the die. Which square does she move her counter to?

b David is on square 2 and moves to –1. What did he throw on the die?

c Greg is on square –6 and moves to –4. What did he throw on the die?

d At one point in the game, David is on –2 and Greg is on –5.

Who is ahead in the game and by how many squares?

You can use a number line to add and subtract positive and negative numbers.

Example 15.3

To work out –3 + 7, go to –3 on the number line and move 7 steps in the + direction (to the right).

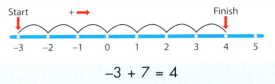

$$-3 + 7 = 4$$

To work out 2 – 5 using the number line, go to 2 on the number line and move 5 steps in the – direction (to the left).

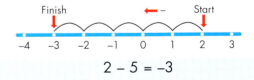

$$2 - 5 = -3$$

Exercise 15d

Use the number line to work out the value of these.
You may need to think beyond the number line after Question 14!

1. 3 − 6
2. −1 + 7
3. −1 − 4
4. −5 + 7
5. +4 − 11
6. 8 − 5
7. −9 + 4
8. +5 − 6
9. 5 − 10
10. −5 − 2
11. +8 − 12
12. −6 + 4
13. 6 − 9 + 3
14. 7 − 14 + 1
15. −5 + 17 − 6
16. −5 − 8 + 3
17. +3 − 14 − 1
18. −10 − 10
19. 8 − 20
20. −100 + 50

Activity 15.3

Activity Sheet 15.3

Exercise 15e

Find the value of these.

1. −10 + 50
2. 7 − 30
3. +4 − 24
4. −17 − 3
5. 9 − 14
6. −25 − 25
7. −15 + 75
8. +20 − 60
9. −24 − 12
10. −6 + 36
11. +11 − 33
12. −40 + 40
13. 42 − 46
14. −15 − 35
15. +400 − 250

Activity 15.4

Activity Sheet 15.4

Discussion 15.4

Using the results of Activity 15.4, can you replace the signs that are next to each other with just one sign in each of these questions?

4 + (−1)   3 − (−2)

Consider the calculation 3 − +2. What is this asking you to do? Can you write this with just one operation to replace − +?

Write down rules for replacing the two signs in each case. Discuss your rules with a partner and decide on a set of rules to follow when adding and subtracting using negative numbers.

Exercise 15f

The first six questions have been started for you. Show full working out for each answer.

1. 2 + −3 = 2 − 3 =
2. −4 − −3 = −4 + 3 =
3. −5 + −8 = −5 − 8 =
4. +3 − +2 = 3 − 2 =
5. 6 − −7 = 6 + 7 =
6. 8 + −3 = 8 − 3 =
7. −5 + −4
8. 6 − +7 =
9. −7 − −7 =
10. + 20 − +5 =
11. −5 + −7 =
12. 9 − 4 =
13. −12 − +6 =
14. +1 + −8 =
15. −6 − 5 =

Activity 15.5

Activity Sheet 15.5

Consolidation Exercise 1

1. Put these values in order, starting with the smallest.

   a   −4   −7   7   −17   −1   17
   b   −8   −9   0   8   −3   −11
   c   −10   −100   −50   −80   −70   −30
   d   4.5   −5.5   5.4   −4.5   −5.4   −4.4
   e   −0.8 −0.5 −0.4   −0.1   −0.6   −0.3

2. The freezing point of a substance is the temperature at which it changes from liquid form to solid form.

   The table shows the freezing point of some substances.

Substance	Freezing point (°C)
Sea water	−1.8
Mercury	−38.9
Nitrogen	−209.86
Water	0
Butter	32
Oxygen	−222.7
Butane	−138

   Put these substances in order, starting with the one that freezes at the highest temperature.

Chapter 15: Negative Numbers

3 Find the answer to these.

a 6 – 10

b –3 + 8

c –10 – 20

d +5 – 9

e –11 + 13

f 7 – 9

g –16 – 8

h –4 – 8 + 17

i +6 – 12 + 4

j –11 + 4 – 1 + 8

k –3 + 7 – 12

l –2 + 3 – 7 + 4

m +5 + 4 – 8 – 9

n –100 + 20 – 80 – 50

o +5 – 15 – 35 + 15

4 Find the answers to these.

The first one is done for you. Set your work out the same way.

a –6 – –7 = –6 + 7 = +1

b +4 – +8 = 4 – 8 =

c 5 + –10 = 5 – 10 =

d –7 + –5 = –7 – 5 =

e 6 – 3 =

f +9 – +11 =

g –12– –6 =

h +10 – 100 =

i 12 + –9 =

j –1 – 0.8 =

5 At 3 am, the temperature of a block of ice was –17.3 °C.

a By 10 am the temperature had increased by 6.8 °C. What was the temperature of the block of ice at 10 am?

b At 8 pm, the temperature of the block of ice was –9.4 °C and at 11 pm it was –11.8 °C. By how many °C had the temperature decreased between 8 pm and 11 pm?

6 Sam's bank balance is –£26.78. The pay for his part time job is £52.36. What is his new bank balance if he deposits all his pay in the bank?

7 A bird is flying at a height of 30.7 metres. A fish is in the sea directly below the bird at a depth of –11.9 metres. What is the difference in height between the bird and the fish?

152

16 Probability

In this chapter, I am learning to:
- recognise situations in which the outcome is uncertain
- use the language of probability
- develop an understanding of probability through practical activities
- understand and use the probability scale from 0 to 1
- calculate the probability of an event happening as a fraction.

Discussion 16.1

In everyday speech we often use the same words to describe the chances of an event happening. Can you suggest other words which could have been used in reply to the question above?

Probability tells us how **likely** an event is to happen. The **likelihood** of an event happening can be shown on a scale.

Activity Sheet 16.1

Activity 16.1

The chances of any event happening are often placed on a scale similar to this one:

Impossible ———————————————————— Certain

What other words to do with probability should we put on the scale and where should they go?

153

Exercise 16a

1. Sarah buys herself a pair of new red shoes.

   Look at each of the following statements and decide which word best describes it. Choose from the following – certain, very likely, even chance, impossible.

   a Both shoes are for her left foot.

   b If she takes a shoe out of the box it will be red.

   c The first shoe Sarah takes out of the box will be for her right foot.

   d Both shoes fit Sarah.

2. Jake tosses a 10 pence coin.

   a What is the likelihood that the coin will land on its edge?

   b Describe the chances of the coin landing tails up.

3. Chloe is playing a card game with these cards.

   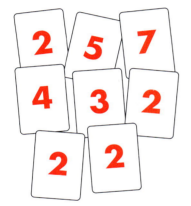

   Choose one of the words below to complete the following sentences.

   impossible, unlikely, evens, likely, certain

   a The chance that Chloe picks a card with the number 2 is _____

   b The chance that Chloe will pick a card with the number 3 is _____

   c The chance that Chloe will pick a card with a number less than 8 is _____

   d The chance that Chloe will pick a card with the number 6 is _____

   e What number is most likely to be on the card that Chloe picks?

Probability is about the **chance** of something happening. The chance of winning can be calculated by looking at the number of possible **outcomes**.

Think of all the television shows where the winner's success depends on chance. Very often people try to win money by doing the Lottery, playing bingo or buying scratch cards. What are the chances of having a winning ticket in the Lottery?

There are nearly 14 million ways to choose six numbers from 1 to 49. There is only one winning combination. This means that there is about 1 chance out of 14 million of winning. As this is a very small amount it is very unlikely to happen!

Example 16.1

When a die is tossed what are the chances of throwing a six?

What are the different outcomes when a die is thrown?

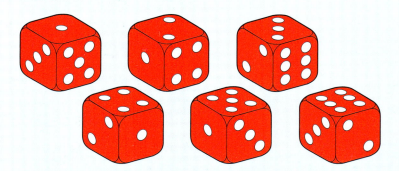

There are six different outcomes. However there is only one way of throwing a six.

Therefore there is only **one chance out of six** of throwing a six.

Example 16.2

There are 20 names in a hat so that one name can be selected **without looking.** There are 12 boys' names and eight girls' names in the hat. Joe is blindfolded and picks out a name.

a What is the chance that a boy's name is picked?

b What is the chance that a girl's name is picked?

There are 20 possible outcomes altogether. There are 12 boys' names so the chance of choosing a boy's name is **12 chances out of 20**.

Similarly for the girls, there are eight girls' names out of a total of 20 possible outcomes. The chance of picking a girl's name is **eight chances out of 20.**

When a choice is made **without looking** this is often referred to as being **at random**.

Chapter 16: Probability

Exercise 16b

1 Copy and complete the statements for each of the events.

Event	Chances of event happening
Throwing a die and scoring an even number	_____ chances out of _____
Picking a red sweet out of a bag containing three green, two blue and three red	_____ chances out of _____
Picking a boy's name out of a class of 12 girls and 15 boys	_____ chances out of _____
Picking the letter H out of the letters in the word CHANCE	_____ chances out of _____
Tossing a coin and getting a tail	_____ chances out of _____

2 In a bag of marbles John counts four red, five blue and one green.

Describe the chance of choosing these.

   a a blue marble

   b a green marble

   c a red marble

   d a black marble

3 The months of the calendar for 2007 are separated and placed in a bag.

If I select a month at random, what are the chances that it will have

   a exactly 28 days

   b 31 days

   c more than 28 days?

4 Hugh has a bag containing two 1p coins, four 2p coins, seven 10p coins and three £1 coins.

He puts his hand in the bag and picks a coin at random.

Write down the chances of selecting each of these coins.

   a 1p   **b** 5p   **c** 10p   **d** £1   **e** 2p   **f** 20p

5 Describe two **different** events where the outcome is:

   a five chances out of 10

   b one chance out of 100

   c three chances out of six

   d one chance out of 30

156

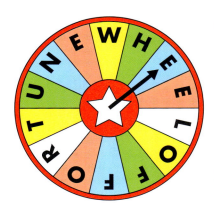

6 Alice and her brother Brian are each given one spin of the wheel. Before they spin they have to say which letter they want the spinner to stop on.

Alice picks the letter O and Brian chooses the letter F.

   a Who has the better chance of winning? Give a reason for your answer.

   b Which letter has the best chance of winning?

7 In a bag of 20 blue counters, what is the chance of picking

   a a white counter?   b a blue counter?

It is more common to describe the chances of an event happening by using fractions. Instead of saying three chances out of four, the probability would be recorded as $\frac{3}{4}$.

Example 16.3

When the spinner is spun once there are eight possible outcomes.

What is the probability of scoring these? a 5 b 1 c 2 d 8

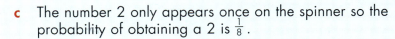

a The number 5 occurs on the spinner twice so there are two chances out of eight of obtaining it. This probability is written as $\frac{2}{8}$ or simplified to $\frac{1}{4}$.

b The number 1 appears on the spinner four times so there are four out of eight chances which is written as $\frac{4}{8}$ or this fraction can be simplified to $\frac{1}{2}$.

c The number 2 only appears once on the spinner so the probability of obtaining a 2 is $\frac{1}{8}$.

d There is no 8 on the spinner so the probability of obtaining an 8 is $\frac{0}{8} = 0$.

Exercise 16c

Give your answers to the probability questions as fractions in their lowest terms.

1 Emmet is playing a card game with these cards. He chooses one card.

  a How many possible outcomes are there?

  b What is the probability of choosing a card with the number 2?

  c What is the probability of choosing a card with the number 5?

  d Which other cards have the same probability of being chosen as a 5?

2 In a game, each player has to spin to see what colour they must stand on.

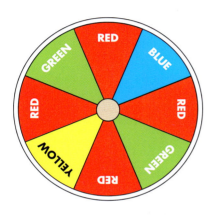

  a John spins the spinner which lands on a colour which has a probability of $\frac{1}{2}$.
  What colour does the spinner land on?

  b The probability of landing on David's colour is $\frac{2}{8}$.
  What colour is David standing on?

  c Which colour is the least likely to be used?

3 In the television game of Winning Balls there are 11 balls to choose from. Three of the balls are loser balls and the other eight are prizes. The prize money is as follows £15 000, £1500, £5000, £2000, £350, £150, £50, £200

  a What is the probability of picking a prize ball of £15 000?

  b What is the probability of winning less than £500?

  c What is the probability of picking a loser ball?

4 Jane has a bag of coloured buttons. There are eight red buttons, five blue buttons and one yellow button.

  She picks a button out of the bag at random.

  a What is the probability that it is yellow?

  b What is the probability that it is red?

  c The probability of choosing a green button is 0. Explain why this is the case.

5 Brian has a bag of 16 marbles. There are only black and blue marbles in the bag. The probability of picking a black marble from the bag is $\frac{3}{8}$.

  a Find out the number of black marbles in the bag.

  b What is the probability of picking a blue marble from the bag?

An event which is impossible has a probability of 0.

An event which is certain to happen has a probability of 1.

Activity 16.2

Activity Sheet 16.2

Activity 16.3

Activity Sheet 16.3

Activity 16.4

Activity Sheet 16.4

Discussion 16.2

When playing games with friends how often do we hear 'That's not fair!'?

On television shows how easy is it to win a big prize?

Are all games fair?

How do the game organisers control the number of big prizes which can be won?

Exercise 16d

SUS16d

A spinner is considered to be fair if all players have an equal chance of winning. To be considered a fair spinner every number, colour or letter should have the same probability of occurring.

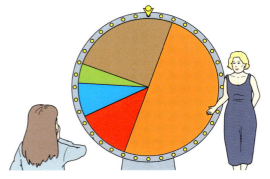

1   Use the spinner to answer these questions.

   a   What is the probability of landing on the orange?

   b   Which colour has a probability of approximately $\frac{1}{4}$?

   c   Which colour has the lowest probability?

   d   Is this a fair spinner? Give a reason for your answer.

2. Look at the game spinners and decide which spinners are fair and which are not. Give reasons for each of your answers.

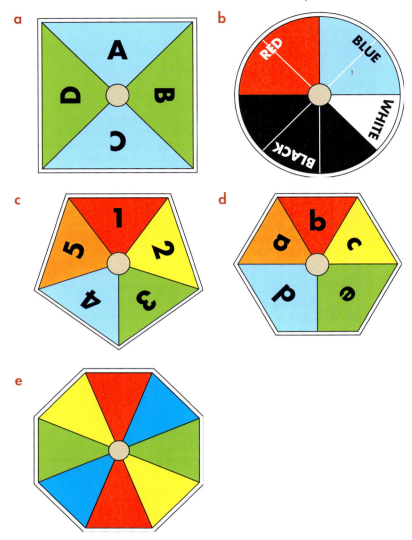

a

b

c

d

e

Compare your answers with others in the class. Do you all agree?

3. A new owner has just bought over the company which makes the spinners used in Question 2. You have been asked to redesign each of the spinners so that they are all fair spinners.

Working in pairs, modify the above spinners so that they are all fair. Use SUS16d.

Carry out practical experiments using the spinners to see if they are fair.

Comment on your findings and compare your results with the rest of the class.

Consolidation Exercise 1

1 Describe the following events using the list of words

impossible, likely, certain, unlikely, even chance.

  a Tomorrow will be 31st June.

  b I will pick a red marble out of a bag containing 10 blue marbles.

  c I will go on holidays to the Moon.

  d I will pick the letter B form the word BLOB.

  e I will have homework tonight.

2 What is the probability of tossing a normal die and obtaining

  a a 6

  b an even number

  c a prime number

  d a multiple of 3

  e a number less than 5

  f a 7?

3 Jim chooses a letter from the word SUCCESSION, at random.

What is the probability that the letter he picks is

  a N   **b** S   **c** a vowel?

4 Valerie has been asked to design a circular spinner with four colours – red, green, blue and yellow.

The chance of scoring blue and yellow must be the same.

Red must have the smallest chance and green must have the greatest chance.

The probability of scoring yellow is $\frac{1}{4}$. Help Valerie by drawing a possible spinner.

5 Jim, John, Julie, Jane, Tanya, Tamara and Thomas each write their names on pieces of paper. All the names are put into a hat. One name is selected at random.

What is the probability that the name picked

  a begins with T   **b** begins with A

  c has six letters   **d** has fewer than five letters?

Task 6: Take Your Pick

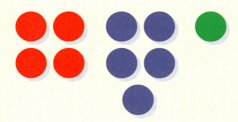

An envelope contains 10 counters.

There are four red, five blue and one green counters.

I pick a counter from the envelope without looking and write down the colour before putting the counter back into the envelope.

If I repeat this experiment 10 times,

a How many red counters should I expect to pick?

b How many blue counters should I expect to pick?

c How many green counters should I expect to pick?

Complete the table on SUSTask6 to show how many of each colour I should expect to pick if I repeat the experiment the given number of times.

The first one has been done for you.

Number of picks	Expected number of counters		
	Red	Blue	Green
10	4	5	1
20			
30			
40			
50			
100			

Now it's your turn to investigate what happens in real life!

The envelope contains

one green, four red and five blue counters.

Take it in turns with your partner to pick out a counter ten times in total.

Place a tally mark on the recording sheet on SUSTask6.

Index

3-D shapes 43–52

A

addition 132, 149–51
algebra 33–42
  division 35
  equations 36–9
  expressions 34–6
  multiplication 35
  substitution 39–40
alternate angles 14–15
angles 12–22
  alternate 14–15
  corresponding 13–14, 17
  exterior 18–19, 21
  interior 15–16, 18–19, 21
  pie charts 2–4, 6
  polygons 19, 21–2
  straight line 17
  supplementary 17
  triangles 18–19, 21
  vertically opposite 12, 17
area 85–7, 107–9

B

bank accounts 147
BODMAS mnemonic 28
body mass index (BMI) 127–8
British Summer Time (BST) 116

C

calculations 23–32
calculators 24, 98, 138
calendars 112
chance 154–9
cones 46
corresponding angles 13–14, 17
cross-sections 45–6, 104–5
cube numbers 23
cube roots 26
cubes/cuboids 102–4
cylinders 46, 49

D

data 2–11
  mean 7–8
  pie charts 2–4, 6
  ranges 9–10
decimals 52–62, 92–101, 132–43
  best usage 94
  decimal places 55–8, 134–6, 138

division 59–60
  equivalences 139
  estimation 54, 59–60
  fractions 92–4, 136–8
  multiplication 54–5, 60–1
  percentages 92–4, 98–9, 137–8
  rounding 53, 55–8, 60
division 35, 59–60
drawing 6, 49–50

E

equations 36–9
equivalences 139
estimation 54, 59–60, 91
expressions 34–6, 39–40
exterior angles 18–19, 21

F

factors 30–1
fairness 159–60
formulae 75–8, 85
fractions 92–101, 132–43
  addition 132
  best usage 94
  calculators 138
  decimals 92–4, 136–8
  equivalences 139
  mixed numbers 136–7
  multiplying 133–6
  percentages 92–4, 137–8
  pie charts 2–4
  probability 157–8
  subtraction 132

G

Greenwich Mean Time (GMT) 114–16
Guideline Daily Amounts (GDA) 128

H

HCF (highest common factor) 30
hemispheres 46
hexagonal pyramids 49
highest common factor (HCF) 30

I

index notation (powers) 23–4
interior angles 15–16, 18–19, 21
International Date Line 116
inverse operations 37–8
isometric dot paper 49–50

L

$l \times b \times h$ volume formula 103–4
LCM (lowest common multiple) 29
likelihood 153–4
lowest common multiple (LCM) 29

M

maps 88
mass 121–31
  body mass 127–30
  imperial units 125–7
  metric units 121–5
  price comparisons 123–5
mean 7–8
measures 82–91, 102–11
  area 85–7, 107–9
  mass 121–7
  perimeter 82–5
  scales 87–9
  volume 102–6
mixed numbers 136–7
multiples 29
multiplication 35, 54–5, 60–1, 133–6

N

negative numbers 144–52
  addition 149–51
  bank accounts 147
  floors in buildings 148
  number lines 144–6, 149–51
  sea depth 148
  subtraction 149–51
  temperature 146–7
nets 50–2
number 23–32
  cube numbers 23
  factors 30–1
  index notation 23–4
  multiples 29
  negative numbers 144–52
  roots 25–6
  square numbers 23
nutrition 128–30

O

octagonal pyramids 49
order of operations 27–9
outcomes 154–9
overtime 137

Index

P

parallel lines 13–17
pentagons 21
percentages 92–101, 132–43
  best usage 94
  calculator key 98
  decimals 92–4, 98–9, 137–8
  equivalences 139
  fractions 92–4, 137–8
perimeter 82–5
pie charts 2–6
planes 48–9
polygons 19, 21–2
polyhedra 48–9
powers (index notation) 23–4
price comparisons 123–5
prime factors 31
prisms 45–6, 49, 104–5
probability 153–62
  chance 154–9
  die tossing 155
  fairness 159–60
  fractions 157–8
  likelihood 153–4
  outcomes 154–9
proportion 68–9, 138
pyramids 47–9

Q

quadrilaterals 19, 21

R

random choice 155
ranges of values 9–10
ratio 63–8
rectangles 22, 85
regular polygons 21
roots 25–6
rounding decimals 53, 55–8, 60,
  134–6

S

savings accounts 139
scales 87–9
sequences 71–81
  differences between terms 71
  formulae 75–8
  rule for next term 71–5
shapes, 3-D 43–52

simplifying expressions 34–6
speed formula 77
spheres 46
square numbers 23
square roots 25
square(-based) pyramids 47
squares, area formula 85
straight line angles 17
substitution 39–40
subtraction 132, 149–51
supplementary angles 17
surface area 85, 107–9

T

temperature 146–7
terms of expressions 34
terms of sequences 71–5
tessellations 22
tetrahedrons 47
three-dimensional (3-D) shapes
  43–52
  drawing 49–50
  nets 50–2
  polyhedra 48–9
  prisms 45–6, 49
  pyramids 47–9
time 112–20
  British Summer Time 116
  calendars 112
  Greenwich Mean Time 114–16
  overtime 137
  timekeeping 117–19
  timetables 112–13
  zones 114–15
tipping 97
transversals 13–17
triangles 18–19, 21, 85

U

unitary ratios 65

V

values of expressions 39–40
vertically opposite angles 12, 17
volume 102–6

Z

zones, time 114–15